International Library of Philosophy and Theology

(MODERN   r)

SARTRE

by

S. U. ZUIDEMA

Translated by Dirk Jellema

1960

THE BAKER BOOK HOUSE
Grand Rapids, Michigan

CONTENTS

Selected Bibliography 6

Author 7

I. Sovereign freedom 9

II. The absurd obstacles to freedom 21

III. Freedom's lordship 26

IV. The check to freedom's lordship 37

V. The dialectic of lordship and failure 42

VI. Exposure and unmasking 50

SELECTED BIBLIOGRAPHY

ESSAYS

L'Imagination (1938)
L'Imaginaire (1940)
Esquisse d'une théorise des émotions (1940)
L'Etre et le Neant (1943)
L'Existentialisme est un humanisme (1947)
L'Engrenage (1948)
Baudelaire (1947)
Situations I, II, III (1947, 1948, 1949)

NOVELS

La Nausée (1938)
La Mur (1939, short stories)
Les Chemins de la liberté (I, L'Age de Raison, 1945;
    II, Le Swisis, 1945; III, La Mort dans l'ame, 1940;
    IV, La Derniére Chance)

PLAYS

Les Mouches (1942)
Huiscles (1940)
La Putain respecteuse (1946)
Morts sans sepultures (1946)
Le Diable et le Bon Dieu (1951)
Nekrassov (1956)

THE AUTHOR

Dr. Siestse Ulbe Zuidema was born in 1906 at Kampen where he attended the *Gereformeerd Gymnasium*. He graduated in 1930 from the Free University of Amsterdam and in 1936 he received his doctorate from that school. His doctoral thesis dealt with *De Wijsbegeerte van Willem van Occum in zijn Commentaar on de Sentenien*.

From 1931-1934 he served as a minister of the Christian Reformed Church of Anna Paulowna Polder. From 1934-1948 he was the minister of the church of Delft for the Mission in Central Java (Dutch East Indies). During 1936-1946 he served as a missionary minister at Soerakarta (Solo) in the Dutch East Indies. During the Second World War, Dr. Zuidema was in a Japanese concentration camp on Java. He returned to Holland in 1946 and became professor in Calvinistic Philosophy in 1948 in the State University of Utrecht and also at the Free University of Amsterdam. Since 1954 he has confined his teaching to the Free University.

Dr. Zuidema is a constant contributor to philosophical and theological journals. His books include: *Nact zonder dagerad, De Mens als historie, Ons Gebed, Ons Christleijke Geloof, Waakt!, Communisme in Ontbinding*.

This monograph on Sartre was translated for the Modern Thinkers Series of the International Library of Philosophy and Theology by Dr. Dirk Jellema, a member of the faculty at Case Institute of Technology, Cleveland.

I. SOVEREIGN FREEDOM

The philosophical thought of Jean-Paul Sartre concerns itself fundamentally with the nature of man. Sartre is interested above all in an accurate portrayal of man, and in the morality which results from such an accurate picture.

Sartre's view of man has as its central point his idea of human freedom. He sees this as a freedom which includes autonomy, self-creation, the creation of values, norms and laws; a freedom which can thus be characterized as man's sovereign self-government and self-rule.

The problem which dominates Sartre's thought, just as it dominates the thought of other existentialists such as Heidegger and Jaspers, is that of delineating the unique way in which man "is." And this is all the more so because Sartre (like his teacher, Heidegger) regards the "being" of man as different from the "being" of everything non-human. He holds that human "being" (which he identifies with human consciousness) is characterized by this: that man's "being" or mode of being, his existence, is always in question, is uncertain, is "in *Frage*." The being of man is thus not so much a possession as a task; not so much a being as a coming; not so much a definition as a question; it is a constant surprise rather than a constant "nature," an adventure· rather than a datum.

It is man who rules his own being, and no one else; man himself, only man, man unrestricted. And as such, man is his own origin, that is, he is so unrestricted in his sovereignty that it can be said that *he elects himself sovereign*, and in this self-election he is independent of everyone and everything. His self-election is the basis for all that he subsequently thinks or does or fails to do. And in a sense it is the basis for everything that happens to him. Man *is* his original self-election; his self-election is his peculiarly human mode of being, and is decisive for all his subsequent behavior and fortune; this act of self-choosing is the basis for all subsequent events and experiences. It is man's *ontological* act — an act which fundamentally determines the being and meaning and destiny of man. Man's

9

existence is the act of a self-election and a self-creation which is underivable, inexplicable, independent, irrefutable, and unjudicable. This act has no ground or basis, and yet it is the basis for all man's life; it is inexplicable, at least by scientific analysis, and yet it lies at the root of all psychology and psychoanalysis as the key to the explanation of much which would otherwise remain a riddle, or remain misunderstood; it owes its power and glory only to itself, and incorporates in principle man's total being; it is not influenced or preceeded by any reasoning, arguments or deliberation, and yet it controls all demonstrations and judgments.

As such, this ontological act of self-choosing is unassailable and indestructible. It is the central point of man's freedom, which must precede all definitions of man's essence, since it is the very thing which defines man's essence: "Existence precedes essence." Possessing this sovereign self-sufficiency, man *is* his freedom, he *is* his *inner* freedom, he *is* his own creator, he *is* his own father.

This dogma of Sartre's may perhaps be called a type of voluntarism, but it should not be forgotten that Sartre himself would protest this, and not without reason. For he feels that the term "free will" is far too weak a description of the freedom of which he is talking. Voluntarism implies that man has a free will to make a choice *after* weighing the "pro's and con's." The freedom which Sartre teaches lies much deeper, and more closely bound with man's very nature. It does not follow rational examination of alternatives, but is already determined, and it dominates and is the basis for all rational examination of alternatives. And it is not something possessed by man, not merely a quality of man's nature; for Sartre, man *is* his freedom, and it is impossible to distinguish between the two, or separate one from the other. Whatever is said about the freedom of man is thereby said about man himself. Man's freedom determines his will.

More precisely stated, Sartre's view of man pictures man as an escape from himself, an *échappement à soi*. This idea seems to be taken over from Nietzsche — whose influence on Sartre is unmistakable, and who influenced Sartre as greatly as Kierkegaard influenced Jaspers. Man must conquer himself, escape from himself, rise above himself; or, as Sartre puts it, he must *transcend* himself. Man is essentially *dynamic*. He can never be at rest, rest is alien, *repos ailleurs;* his "being" is a "becoming"; his freedom consists in large part that he can never and nowhere come to a stop; he cannot and he may not. "Hence man is that which he is not, and when he is, he is nothing." Rest is not a mere halt or recession; it is decay, decadence, deterioration; it is treason against freedom, and treason against himself. Man is pilgrim, always on the way to something else, a builder of something else, an architect; someone who is always ahead of himself, or — seen from another point of view — always behind himself.

This is related to the "fact" that man is not complete. Man is a lack, a shortage, a *totalité détotalisée*, a whole which does not yet exist — but which will come, and which already dominates the lack. The task of man is thus one of self-cultivation, self-development, self-creation, self-completion. Man is only when he is dead; until then he is "becoming." And when he is dead, he is not his real self. His freedom is gone; what "was" existence has not become "essence"; after death, he *is* simply what he was and what he will be; he has finally become the same as himself, identical with himself; and thus he is no longer truly human.

Freedom in Sartre's sense (that man *is* freedom) implies just this, that man may never become identical with himself, may never "be"; man is "becoming," not "being"; dynamic, not static. That man is *sovereign* freedom means that man owes this "becoming" to his own efforts, to his own self, and that man "possesses" a mode of existence like that which theologians call continual creation *(creatio continuata)*. Man continually constitutes himself in continual renewals, continual innovations. He escapes from himself by approaching himself; he escapes from (the incomplete) himself by approaching (the complete) himself; and he approaches himself by escaping from himself. He is the unity of his own past and present and future; since in this approach to himself which he makes by continually renewing himself, he takes up in the present his own past, by a free act, and carries it with him towards the future which he is creating by his present acts. If man became identical with himself, he would be identical with his past, and determined by this past; and that would mean the end of his sovereignty and freedom. But due to the "fact" that he can *temporalize* himself, he can retain his sovereignty and freedom. That is, by a unique creative free act of unification, he acts in the present to carry his past along with him to the future. And thus he can both escape himself and take himself with him; he can at the same time both accept himself and creatively and radically reconstruct himself. Man's existence is the building of the self, self-cultivation, and man is at the same time material and product, builder and material, worker and planner in one and the same person, in service to himself and master of himself. Without any right to vacation, but without fear of being unemployed; with never a shortage of material or a lack of work; but also without the possibility of being a mere spectator. For then man would retire from the obligations of his freedom, and thereby deceive himself into thinking that this retirement and the resultant unemployment can be maintained by some means other than the exercise of the freedom he is trying to escape. That is, he would deceive himself against his own better knowledge into believing that freedom can be escaped by denying its existence, and that sovereignty can be avoided by refusing to admit that there is such a thing. Actually, such a man is only misusing his freedom, and even that misuse can be maintained only by using the very freedom and sovereignty which are being denied. The spectator is also, willy-nilly, a builder; busy, despite his protests, in self-cultivation; even though the self-cultivation partakes of the fraudulant.

Man is thus "doomed to be free." His freedom is unconditional and inescapable, impregnable and inevitable. His sovereignty is so inalienable that he himself cannot give it away.

Sartre is an extreme individualist. His freedom is the freedom of the individual. Sartre's philosophy of freedom abstracts man from all social relationships and bonds; and he thus has to face the problem of explaining why social bonds and relationships do in fact exist, despite the "fact" that every man in principle isolates himself as the unique absolute and the absolute unique, in his own hermetically sealed realm of freedom, an imperialistic realm of freedom.

Sartre's view of man is completely opposed to that of the Bible. Sartre wants nothing to do with the basic law of love for God and one's neighbor. This law, for him, is in open conflict with the existential "law of being" which man must hold to: that is, the norm and the ideal of being his true self, of becoming himself, choosing himself, designing and building and developing himself, reaching himself and possessing himself. Freedom is the bulwark of the self-isolating man, and any attempt to break down this bulwark by supporting man-in-relationship is, in Sartre's eyes, treason against man, man's self-betrayal.

The only permissable relationship to another man, to the "Other," is that of the aggressor, attempting to broaden one's own might and power of sovereign freedom to include the Other; to dominate him and exploit him and use him in one's own struggle to find one's self as the basis for being.

Gabriel Marcel, whose philosophy of *disponsibility* is, on this point, the complete opposite of Sartre's, rightly remarks that Sartre's individualistic idea of freedom is an attempt to find a justification for a fundamentally irreligious unavailability, or refusal to serve; Sartre's free man may never make himself available for service to a fellow

12

man, or to the community, or to God. But he does have the duty and the call to practice auto-eroticism: to love himself above all, to love himself alone, to love himself as freedom and the might and power of freedom. An irreligious solipsism, inseparably connected with his idea of freedom, lies at the root of Sartre's philosophy of man.

This rigorous individualism, steeped in an almost sexual auto-eroticism, brings Sartre to oppose Christianity, humanism, and Marxism. As regards politics, he is — naturally! — the philosopher of *anarchism*, which calls trust in others treason, and which actually honors lack of trust by making a heroic virtue of "trust" in the individual's isolated freedom, and in that alone. It appears to me that there are here made evident undeniable relationships between Sartre's thought and the ideas of a *decadent* bourgeoisie.

The reverse side of Sartre's extreme individualistic dogma of freedom is that man is forever thrown back on himself, abandoned to himself, can expect good only from himself, stands in relationship only to himself. In this isolation, he finds his power, and irrevocable abandonment.

Sartre bases this irreligious and amoral view of man on an ontology of man, in a view of being, in an existentialist anthropology.

According to his teaching, the "essence" of that freedom which man *is*, is nothing else than annihilation, *nihilation* (neantisation). The being of man consists of a not-being and in a nihilation[1]) of that which is. The freedom which man is, which constitutes man, finds its basis in the human act of nihilation. By this act of nihilation, man separates himself from his environment, from the world around him, from the men around him, from his own past, from himself as he was up to now. It is because of this act of nihilation, which separates man from that which surrounds him, that it can be said that "man is not what he is, and he is what he is not." Because of that act, his identity with himself vanishes, and his relations with his environment, and indeed every relationship. Man is in relation to all else an act of nihilation, and the freedom of man is the fruit of this relation, this *relation of nullity*. And man stands in this relation with himself too. Between man and his surroundings, between man and his own past, there stands a wall, built by man himself; an iron wall of nothingness and nihilation. Man is radically separate being, whose every essence is this nihilation, this self-isolation, this "null-point existence." It is be-

---

[1]) The term used by Sartre "neantisation" is translated throughout by the term nihilation. It is to be hoped that its peculiar meaning will be clear from the context. DHF

cause of this nihilation that man can be truly free, and enjoy complete autonomy, and be completely "within" himself. Man *is* this act of *nihilation*, repeated time and again; he is this inner and centripetal act; he is imprisoned within himself and by himself, and no man can break down these prison walls, these walls of nihilation of all relationships.

Actually, then, Sartre's ontology of man is the opposite of an ontology; it is not an idea of "being," but rather of "non-being"; it is a non-ontology, a *mè-ontologia*, based not on being but on nothingness and annihilation. The life and the struggle of man, man's true existence, is not a *real-ization*, a realization, but rather a *dis-realization;* his becoming is an un-becoming, his self-creation a disruption, and his self-cultivation a destruction.

Nihilation is then the basis for the freedom which man is. Man, when seen from an ontological standpoint, is thus a lessening of being, a weakening of being, a low point, a gap in the structure of being, a *décompression d'être,* something insubstantial, something deficient. When man comes into the world, is Nothing, and Nihilation which come into the world; nothing more and nothing less. Man is the relation of nullity, *le rapport nul,* and it is in this being-less mode of being, that there lies his freedom from everything which has being. Man's freedom — and thus man himself — is *absolute,* since it is unlimited by any relationships or dependence on relationships.

Every nihilation is by its very structure a grounding, a foundation; but this foundational characteristic of nihilation can be explained only in paradoxes. For the foundation laid by nihilation is an abyss, a "gap in being." In his nihilating act of freedom, man gives to himself *aseitas,* being outside himself and within himself; but this *aseitas* has no existence, it has no being, it is the nihilation of being. Thus the self-creation of man can take place only in a self-nihilation, a nihilation of being, in the forming of an abyss, in the creation of a distance, in the construction of an identity which is constantly denied, a coinciding constantly prevented from occurring. Because of this nihilating foundation, man is not what he is, is never what he is; and he can lift himself above being, and create nothingness as the abyss-like foundation for his own sovereign completeness and impregnability. Man lays the foundation for himself; not in his essential being, but in his essential non-being. He is not his own being, but rather nihilates his own being, again and again finds his own not-being, acts as a nihilating thing which (judged from the standpoint of his "being") is *outside* himself. Man's immanence is his transcendence; he is himself only when he is not himself. This nihilation is the basis for

14

his surpassing himself and transcending himself; it is the abyss in which he can constantly separate himself from his own past "being," and thus emerge again to freedom.

The creative freedom of man, then, is a *nihilistic* act of freedom; not a realization but a dis-realization, the founding of the nihilation of himself, and only thus a self-creation and a self-founding. With man comes Nothing into the world of being, and with Nothing the self-nihilating and self-isolating separateness of man, the founding of man as the empty and insubstantial non-being which has no relation to anything else. This is due to the iron ring of nihilation with which man surrounds himself and continually surrounds himself again and again; so that man is not of this world, since he is not; he is nothing, and he himself lays the foundation for his own non-being.

In order to characterize the inner relationship in Sartre's thought between his existentialism and this nihilistic view of man, Mounnier wittily remarks that Sartre's existentialism is actually an "inexistentialism," a presentation of not-being and non-existence as "essential" components of human existence and essence and being.

Sartre pays dearly for his *sovereignty* of man; the price he pays is *nihilism*. Man is his own basis, his own grounding; but only because he is the basis for his own self-nihilation, and since he is his own nihilating and annihilating ground and basis, he is the basis for non-being. Man's sovereignty cannot "be," it has no being, it is Nothing, *le Neant;* his self-creation is a self-nihilation, his self-cultivation a destruction. Thus the *cult* of man in Sartre, the worship of man's sovereign freedom, is paired with an outlook on *culture* which reduces man's cultural task to the nihilation of being, and narrows his cultural calling to that of self-culture, and that means the nihilation of the last bonds between the individual and objective reality, and thus dis-realization. This "inner" and existential act of dis-realization is the dominating principle of Sartre's view of man, and indeed of his whole outlook on life and the world. The *divine* sovereignty which Sartre takes from God and gives to man becomes *demonized* and perverted into a creative idea of culture, in which self-culture means self-nihilating; and in which the only thing man creates is his own self-existence, his self's being; and even this is not "self" insofar as it is, and insofar as it is true "self," it is not.

Sartre's idea of human sovereignty is thus intimately related to his undermining of the idea of man's being; man's self-possession, self-rule and self-election go hand in hand with his self-alienation.

But the only passion which seems to inspire Sartre is the passion for man's sovereignty; the lust for self-election, self-rule, the autonomous

15

man, rooted in an unlimited self-love, in an erotically-tinted self-love, in auto-eroticism.

This appears with especial clarity in Sartre's treatment of *anxiety* and the experience of anxiety.

The "ontological" experience of anxiety which Sartre takes up is, he says, a specifically qualified means of ontological revelation. For while this experience of anxiety does not lay bare the character of being, or of anything in the objective world, still it does disclose the nature of the self, and in particular the nihilating character of the self. Anxiety reveals the depth of the self's uneasiness regarding the certainty of the self, the retention of the self's nihilating and sovereign character. Nothing could be so terrible as the self-alienation of man. And this self-alienation reaches its full realization whenever man and his continually recurring act of freedom becomes dominated either by the fiction of a belief in God, or by the actuality of the world of being (the objective world). This world means the lost of man's own subjectivity, and the complete objectivizing of man's nature. It would mean the reduction of man to something which is, something which has being; the reduction of man to the mode of being which things have; the reduction to a thing *(la chose)*.

In the ontological experience of anxiety, man is called back to himself by the abyss of sovereign non-being; back to the carrying out of the one truly human task, self-cultivation through the nihilation of being. In this experience of anxiety man becomes warned by his own nihilating base and foundation; warned of threatening danger, the danger that he might coincide with himself, and should simply be what he is, and thus no longer have a "self." Sartre's teachings about man's sovereign freedom are thus reinforced by this experience of anxiety, the fear of self-alienation, the loss of self, the loss of freedom; the "existential persecution complex." Sartre's attack on the "normal man" and the social leanings of the normal man is prompted by his unhealthy affection for the abnormal man, who feels himself deceived and waylaid and persecuted, and who regards himself as wholly normal in having such feelings. One can note already the working out of Sartre's idea of man's self as an unhappy consciousness *(conscience malheureuse)* in an unhappy state *(état malheureux)*. The uncertainty and the fragility of man's power of freedom, the anxiety over the possible loss of freedom — these nourish Sartre's hybrid idea of man's sovereign freedom as the unconquerable fortress of innerness and subjectivity.

This "ontological" anxiety reveals to the individual man — and to this philosophy of man — something which would otherwise remain hidden and unknowable; that is, the deepest level of the origin of man, the root of man's existence; man's sovereign nihilating freedom, his self-becoming. Thus Sartre's whole philosophy of freedom, and the infallibility of his ontological interpretation of anxiety, rests on the infallibility of this experience of anxiety. Anxiety reveals to man his highest good and his dearest possession, his freedom, his self-rule, his self-being in the nihilating act of complete subjectivity, his self-immanence. This act of freedom is (as will appear in more detail below) an act which may be denied, but never escaped; an act which is "given" with the "fact" of man's existence, and as such a "contingent" given cannot be annihilated as a fact. "We are condemned to freedom."

The *directrix* for every human act of freedom, says Sartre, is the *transcendence* of man over himself and over being. And this directrix, this guiding principle, is also based on the ontology of man.

Man is on the way toward himself and toward self-existence. He *is* himself only incompletely. For self-existence is not, considered as (self) existence, an act of freedom or a sovereign self; and self-existence considered as self (existence) is more than something which merely exists, which *is*; it is active *transcending* itself, reaching beyond itself, surpassing itself, escaping itself; it is not an "is," a being, but rather a becoming, or indeed an "un-becoming."

The *self* of man is based on nihilation, on man's ontological act of freedom; and it is thus that man is his own founder, his own creator. But this is true only in the context of nihilation, not in any positive or being-creating sense. Man is nothing more than a gap in the structure of being, and insofar as the self allows itself merely to *be*, to that extent it loses the power to be its own source and its own explanation, its own basis and its own creator. This ontological *lack* of being (though the source of man's sovereign freedom) threatens to overwhelm man. So man is called to the task, and his self-development is guided by the ideal, of being himself in a special sense; being himself without basing this being on anything outside man's power or control; for all such things are therefore (!) not "real." This is possible only if man can overcome contingency and contingent being, being which depends on something else, and create himself as a self-being, a self-contained being; a being which can base not only its self-nihilation (through the recurring ontological act of freedom) but also its self-existence, its self-*being* on itself. The ideal to be reached is thus that of *sovereign being;* being which depends on nothing outside itself, and is hence truly sovereign; and being which because of this can never be annihilated, and thus is true being.

The task of transcendence, therefore, has two aspects. First, to transcend the self considered as simple nihilation of being; and second, to transcend the contingency of (objective) being, the dependence and meaninglessness of all being outside man's sovereign freedom, which alone can act in a foundational and meaningful manner.

Hence the unique existential act of man can be described as that act which aims at overcoming, first, the ontological lack of being in man's self, and second, the contingency and meaninglessness of all (objective) being. Man is thus on the way to truly sovereign being, in which he *is* his freedom, and in which his freedom can cast off the nihilation which is its basis.

Man is on the road to self-being, self-existence; on the road to overcoming (with the help of nihilation, which makes his act of freedom possible) the self's "un-becoming," without losing the act of freedom; on the road to the identification of "being" and "self." *Man is his struggle.* But this ideal, this ontological and thus inelectable ideal, this project which concerns the very structure of man's being, and which can be viewed as the innermost desire of man — this ideal is unattainable. For the act of freedom can exist only by the grace of nihilation, and being can no longer be being unless it coincides with itself and at the same time is different from itself — and this is precluded by the nature of freedom. Thus the directrix of transcendence (used always in the active sense, meaning to transcend) is nothing else than an *illusion,* and man's passion for freedom is a *useless* passion, and man's self-development is an *échec,* a contradiction, doomed to failure. But despite all this, it is still the only directrix, the only guiding principle, proper to human freedom. And the finiteness of all man's subjective activity spurs on this activity, spurs it on to pursue this eternal ideal of self-being, in the heroic consciousness that this ideal and this hunt will lead to. . . *nothing.*

Whatever may miscarry and go wrong, even though it be the entire praxis of man's existence and struggle, there is one thing which remains untouched: the sovereignty of man's freedom and man's sovereign struggle to transcend himself. It is this *unending struggle* which gives glory to man's life; to his projects and acts, and also to the miscarriage and failure of his life. The portion of man, the destiny of man, is life, the realization of the existential struggle, the expansion of man's freedom as he reaches for complete self-existence; and man finds this meaning in the sovereign freedom that he "is." The cult of self does not disappear even though self-culture and self-development are seen to be fruitless.

As is the case in all existentialist thought, Sartre's philosophy of freedom is closely related to his philosophy of *reflection*. The essential meaning of freedom can be seen only in its intimate relation to the *idea* of freedom. Existence is regarded by many existentialist not only as a subjective *act*, but also as subjective reflection about this act, and the two aspects cannot be separated from each other.

Free existence, self-being, is at the same time self-consciousness. So Sartre often calls the self simply consciousness, *conscience*. And he goes on to say that this consciousness is of such a nature that although it is the purest subjectivity, it does not objectify freedom; it does not reduce it to a thing.

This starting-point is referred to by Sartre when he speaks of that existential *"pure* reflection" which our consciousness should be. Man's self-consciousness is, as pure reflection, consciousness about *itself*, about man's subjective act of freedom; and this means that every man has himself as a mirror-image, that he can be present with himself and view himself, without thereby separating himself from himself. Self-consciousness is a self-presentation, which at the same time separates the self from itself and does not do so. It is a mirror-image which is viewed by the self, it is before the viewing self, it is a *pour-soi;* but a mirror-image which coincides and is the same as the self, and the self's ontological act of freedom. This self-picturing of man which is identical with his sovereign act of freedom is thus a self-picturing which is not really reflection in the usual sense; for the mirror-image is identical with the viewer. Man is, to use Descartes' term, a *cogito préréflexif*, a self-consciousness which *is* the self; *conscience-soi* rather than *conscience de soi*, self-consciousness rather than consciousness about the self.

Thus this existential reflection is in a sense the same as the existential act of freedom; and the existential act of freedom is never without existential reflection. The self *is* self-consciousness.

The philosophy of freedom found in Sartre is thus at the same time a philosophy of consciousness. Human subjectivity is consciousness and the existential act of freedom rolled into one.

As such, our consciousness is inexplicable by and inaccessible to science and objectivizing knowledge. Man's reason cannot capture self-consciousness and the act of freedom in its field of vision, and thus neither can occupy in a scientific reason. These subjective things withdraw themselves and avoid any scientific analysis or scientific formulation. Freedom does not let itself be determined; it would then cease to be freedom. The essence of man lies deeper than science can penetrate. And as pure sovereign subjectivity, it does not allow itself to be objectivized, to become a field for scientific analysis. Indeed, the existential act, the act of freedom, precedes every decision of the will, and thus precedes every rational examination. As sovereign freedom, it rules itself; it protects its own inaccessability, and keeps the scientific investigator outside the bounds of its subjectivity. Reason is powerless to incorporate man's "being" or even to examine it. The existential nature of man is irrational sovereign freedom. Thus existentialism disposes with philosophical positivism and its trust in science; and also of neo-positivism and neo-idealism.

Sartre has taken the humanistic belief in the freedom of man and radicalized it; but at the same time he has made it look nonsensical. For Sartre, the freedom of man is so basic and so radical that man *is* his freedom and the act of freedom. There is nothing human which lies outside or beyond this free being. But at the same time, this free being is so completely surrounded by nothingness and illusion that it is robbed of all positive meaning. Sartre's philosophy is above all a philosophy of this openly anti-religious and anti-Christian idea of freedom. Without this view of freedom, Sartre's picture of man would fall to pieces. Sartre clothes man in God's sovereignty, and tells him that he is absolute. Man's glory is divine glory; his "essence" is divine; his origin and existence is found in his choice for freedom. Thus the self-worship of man reaches a terrifying height in Sartre. He must pay a price for his irreligious self-deification of man; and the price he pays is the demonization of this deification, and the demonization of man. And this leads to the violation of humanistic faith in man. For the meaning of man's life becomes an illusion; man's life is characterized by failure; and the basis of man's sovereignty is nothingness. The being of man as dis-realization is the opposite of what scholastic theology teaches about the being of God. The glorious human struggle for freedom and culture oscillates between nihilism and illusionism. Man transcends nothingness only to reach something which is less than nothingness; an illusion. An illusion; an impossible idea, a mirage, which man recognizes to be a mirage, and yet a mirage which man must follow if he is not to give up his sovereignty, his drive for sovereignty. Man is at best a miscarriage, a failure. He is that in his auto-eroticism, in his hermetically-sealed self-love, in his authentic essence. In Sartre's existentialism, then, humanism has developed into a full-blown anti-humanism. And just as existentialism is really anti-existentialism, so this type of humanism with its self-deification of man is actually a self-demonization of man. And how could it be otherwise? — for everything which has being is contingent and therefore (!) meaningless, and the meaning of the world and of

20

man must thus rest on what is-not, on nothingness, on annihilation, on the nihilating power of man. Sartre's irreligious philosophy takes away all positive meaning from cult and culture, from religion and work; and the man whom Sartre has left is thus the hollow man.

When the last bands which related humanism to Christianity are cut, as Sartre cuts them, then humanism can no longer be distinguished from anti-humanism, or man from a demon, or the world from hell. The Christian knows what Sartre does not: that the self-alienation of man lies in his self-worship.

II. THE ABSURD OBSTACLES TO FREEDOM

Sartre supports not only the philosophical idealism of freedom, tinged as his version is with nihilism and existentialism, but also the sovereignty of human subjectivism. In this respect he partially follows Fichte. But Sartre does not adopt the absolute idealism of freedom which is Fichte's. The existence of objective reality does not depend, in Sartre, on the self-positing of the human or divine subject. And non-human reality is not, for Sartre, simply material which is used by the "absolute" ego for its reasoned and autonomous task of freedom; not simply something which the "absolute" ego places over against itself purposely as an obstacle which must be overcome. For Sartre, the non-human − and for him this means everything which cannot "be" consciousness − gives neither existence nor meaning to sovereign human freedom.

The ego does not *posit* the objective world; on the contrary, the human ego reveals its sovereignty by *nihilating* the objective world. Objective reality, that which is independent of the human act of freedom, simply *is*. For Sartre, objective reality is something completely different and alien from the existential act of freedom. Sartre does hold that "meaning" and "basis" can be found only in the human act of freedom, and this is a dogma of all idealisms of freedom. But he also says − and in contrast to Fichte − that non-human actually has no intimate relation to human self-actualization, and hence *must* be contingent and meaningless, a. product of chance, with no ground, completely gratuitous, capricious and arbitrary, "too much;" chaotic and absurd.

Thus Sartre, in his treatment of non-subjective existence, takes a position different from the absolute and complete idealism associated with Fichte. He develops his own position through his treatment of the idea of *contingency*.

"Contingent" means, for Sartre, anything whose origin and existence cannot be deduced from or reduced to man's existential and ontological act of freedom. Everything which is contingent has no ground for being, no meaning, and lacks all relationship to the meaning-creating act of freedom, and thus can find origin and existence only in "original chaos." Sartre uses the words "contingency," "chaos," and "absurdity" as synonyms. These words express the complete arbitrariness and aimlessness, the *gratuité parfait* of everything not related to the existential act of freedom.

Three things might be noted in connection with Sartre's idea of contingency: first, Sartre's radicalizing of the nihilating existential act of freedom into the only meaningful and meaning-creating thing in the world. Whatever falls outside of it, whatever "is" not this nihilating freedom, is necessarily contingent, meaningless and foundationless. Sartre's choice for a philosophy of freedom and his partiality for the "glory" of man show themselves very clearly in this characterization of everything not specifically included in man's sovereign objectivity. Sartre teaches, as do other philosophers of the idealism of freedom, that man and only man gives meaning to non-human reality. He will hear nothing of a divine plan, of divine ordinances, of divine providence, or of divine rule. All reality which lies outside of man's subjective act of freedom can be nothing else than absurd; it is a chaos, not a cosmos; it is absurd and hideous, hateful, irritating, and superfluous.

Secondly, it should be noted that Sartre refuses to accept any rationalistic view of the universe which would hold that non-subjective reality is meaningful, and that this meaningfulness is characterized by orderliness, physical law, and susceptibility to scientific analysis. Sartre does not shrink from admitting occasionally that non-human reality is determined, bound by a universal determinism, and thereby subject to scientific analysis and control. He does not oppose positivism on that point. But, says he, this does not affect the fundamental irrationality and contingency of non-human reality. It could escape irrationality and contingency only if it had its origin and basis in man's creative freedom; and this, of course, is not the case.

Then, too, we should distinguish carefully between contingency and freedom. Sartre's idea of contingency depends on his idea of freedom. Non-human reality is contingent because it is not free. It does not originate itself or limit itself, and it is not based on man's freedom. Therefore contingency is meaningless, while freedom is meaningful and meaning-creating. Hence contingency has no basis, while freedom creates a basis; hence contingency is eternal, while freedom temporalizes; hence contingency is brute, naked being, while the act of freedom nihilates being. Contingent reality and the free consciousness of man are related as "being" and "nothingness," as *être* and *néant* (the title of Sartre's main work).

The structure of contingent reality, of "being," is that it "is"; nothing more and nothing less. One can say no more about it, and indeed even to say that much is already saying too much. For that describes the "being" of being; and brute being, contingent reality, has no being which can be described. Contingent being has no notions; and it should have no notions.

Sartre calls contingent being "in-itself" *(en-soi)*, in contrast to the *pour-soi* or mirror-image character of consciousness. Contingent being knows no self-differentiation, for it is bare of any self-being, and thus bare of any relation to itself. It is what it is, period. A huge, compact, full, undifferentiated mass of being which — but we are already saying more than we should about it — coincides with itself; and as fact, as actuality, as positive being, it knows no *pour-soi*. It is a brute fact, a *fait brut*, and that is all it is.

In his sense it is absolute; without any internal relation with man's meaning-giving act of freedom, and totally different from man.

Reference can well be made at this point to Sartre's *materialism*. This refers to the fact that Sartre (as opposed to, e.g., Fichte) does not derive the being of the non-human world from the ego's act of freedom. Being is rather an alien obstacle to the human ego, a thing whose origin cannot be known and which surely cannot be derived from the human ego; indeed, it has no origin, it is absurd, and has no basis. It stands over against man as something alien and other.

It is so alien, says Sartre, that all control of it, and all differentiation within it, is the product of man's work of freedom. And thus such differentiation is unreal and not actual, since man in his thought and deed can only dis-actualize and dis-realize. The reality which non-human being has is thus limited, according to Sartre, to the reality which remains after human impositions and constructions have been removed from it. Sartre's objective reality thus is made up of the natural aspects of non-human reality, the unrevised, unpolished, chaotic aspects. In this sense it is correct to speak of the materialism of Sartre's view of non-human reality.

The "reality" of objective being, just as the "reality" (!) of man's free consciousness, has a special means of revealing itself to man. Objective reality reveals itself to us in the experience of *nausea*. This comes to us whenever we lose the nihilating distancing of the act of freedom, and thus are threatened with incorporation in the realm of mere being. Sartre wrote about this experience of nausea in one of his earliest works, *La Nausée.* Being reveals itself to us, in this experience, in all its chaotic, useless, baseless, absurd, brute factuality.

This experience and its meaning is the opposite of the experience of anxiety and its meaning. It reveals to us that which we, as an ontological act of freedom, in the core of our existence, are not; inexplicable, irrational, superfluous reality. It reveals to us, in this ontological experience of being, the opposite of our self-existence; the absolute, which we are not. And in this nausea which meaningless contingency arouses in us, we "affirm" in an ontological, pre-reflexive, existential experience, that we cannot make this "being" vanish, but that it is there, in contrast to us. We also discover, in the nausea aroused through this revelation of being, in a pre-reflexive and existential fashion that we do not want to be that kind of being; anything but that. And we discover implicity and indirectly the self-isolation available throught the act of nihilation, which is the basis for our self-becoming, our self-separation from this "nauseating" reality. Being may be one thing and everything; well, we are not *that;* aversion is born; man is born as aversion. He exists as "anything but that!" He exists as an annihilator of "that." His aversion is above all for the contingency of being, its impotence to create its own basis, its "naked" factuality. And this is because man, as nihilation, demands a freedom which can create its own basis, and which governs its own origin and aims. "In any event not contingent, not absurd, not brute fact and nothing besides" — that is the slogan which directs every human activity, and which is the law for everything truly human in man.

Being and not-being, being and consciousness, contingency and freedom, to be identical with self and dialectically to escape self — these opposite poles repel each other, preclude each other, and form the "essence" of both the non-human and the human. The being of being and the "being" of man are completely different from each other. They are so completely different that the terms "being" (of the world) and "being" (of man), even though they are homonymous and univocal, have no inner likeness, and represent not even analogous forms of being, no *analogia entis.* Being and consciousness, world and man; these are two realms which do not correspond, which have no inner resemblence, which stand opposed to each other. The ontology of being is totally different from the ontology of consciousness. Man is alienated from the world, and the world alienated from man. Man stands in the world as an alien being from afar, and for man the world is a closed world, an intractable opponent of man's ontological act of freedom.

In Hegel's dialectic of being, spirit throws itself against its opposite, and becomes nature; so that it can as nature throw itself against its opposite, and become spirit-nature. The thesis of spirit throws itself against its antithesis, in order to be reconciled in unity, in the synthesis of thesis and antithesis.

Such an idealistic-dialectic view of being cannot be found in Sartre. To begin with, he teaches that it is not consciousness or spirit which is primary, but rather being, nature. The *factuality* of freedom precedes freedom; we are doomed to freedom. Our acts of freedom are self-founding and foundational; but the *being* of the self- the being of the act of freedom, is contingent. And without this contingent factuality there can be no act of freedom. Man is a "gap in the structure of being," and if being should vanish, so would the being-nihilating character of our existential act of freedom. But if our act of freedom should disappear, if the humanity of man should vanish, objective reality would not; it would endure to eternity in its brute fashion, for it "is."

Hence man's nihilation of being is nihilated being, escaped from being, which can escape from being only as long as it does not escape completely. In this sense, man *is being*, identical with being, he *is* a thing, *la chose*, he *is* his body; only an unreal distance then separates him from objective reality. His transcending of being can never leave the ground, can never leave the starting line, can never "in fact" loose itself from being. Only being "is." Man "is" more than his body, and consciousness "is" more than being, but nevertheless only in the measure that man *is* his body. In a sense he is his body; not the material of his body, but still his body only to the extent that he does at the same time coincide with the material.

And insofar as he is not reality, insofar as he refuses to be mere brute being, he can refuse only by becoming a *décompression d'être*, a lessening of the compact massiveness of being, a hollow and emptiness in the fullness of being, a relation of nullity.

All of this shows the dominance exercised by being, and the obstacles in the way of sovereign freedom. These are not obstacles which exercise sovereignty over freedom, but they are still obstacles which loom up even before freedom is "born"; they are the eternal, and the eternal becomes an obstacle to freedom and its *temporalizing* effect.

Ideologically and axiologically, only sovereign freedom prevails. Being is less worthy, unworthy; it arouses aversion, it is contingent. Yet *ontologically* speaking it recaptures its primacy, for it is the eternal, the only thing which is, and it lies at the basis of the existential acts of freedom; it "is" as pure contingency, pure determinacy, and it is nothing more than that. And thus, even though ontologically primary, it can, ontologically speaking, put no weight in the scale.

There is nothing left here of an idealistic dialectic. There is nothing of an Hegelian higher synthesis between being and consciousness, nature and spirit. Sartre knows no synthesis. It is true that spirit, consciousness, takes the lead in the attempt to bridge the gap between freedom and contingency, the attempt to create a self, by transcending the self, which will be a unity of "self" and "being," of *pour-soi* and *en-soi*. But this synthesis is foredoomed to failure; it is an *illusion*. True synthesis is absent. Being does not allow itself to be dis-realized; or, better, it does not tolerate any attempt to ground it, to base it. The obstacles to freedom are unconquerable, and man is a *useless* passion, a struggle with no attainable end.

There must be considered, in addition, the "brute fact" of death. Death does not allow itself to be incorporated in the realm of the existential act of freedom. It comes with overpowering strength from somewhere beyond, and it "dis-realizes" or "dis-actualizes" man's struggle to use freedom to "dis-realize" being, and to develop his self. Death puts an end to the temporalizing effect of man's freedom, puts an end to man's consciousness and his nihilation of objective being. After death, man, in the most complete sense, *is*. He is *en-soi*, he is a *thing*, he is contingent, he is identical with himself. Man's drive for complete sovereignty stops. "Where the tree falls, there it lies."

Sartre's existentialism can best be evaluated, in my opinion, by comparing it with Fichte's idealism of freedom. From Fichte, he takes his outlook regarding man's sovereign freedom and man's subjectivity. But in contrast to Fichte (and Hegel), he sees objective reality as an independent pole over against man's spirit. The antithesis between the freedom of consciousness and the being of reality is radicalized. Thus it is not surprising that a synthesis between them can be had only in the sense of an illusory synthesis; there is no *Vermittlung*, no "eschatology" of completion. Man's destiny is his unhappy consciousness, his *conscience malheureuse*, and death is his abrupt and absurd end. Only the *unending* struggle of the existential act of freedom is saved from this demolition of previous idealistic philosophies of freedom. The plot of the drama in which this unending struggle plays its fruitless role is one of danger, risk, tension, fragility, and ruin. Man gains the prize of honor by keeping up this struggle to the end, with the motto *Ut desint vires, tamen est laudanda voluntas* — even if strength fails, the wish is laudable. Man is a ship doomed to sink into the sea of eternal being, and that is the final destiny of all his self development.

III. FREEDOM'S LORDSHIP

It is in the "ontological" and existential experience of anxiety that man discovers his own freedom, his own responsibility to freedom, and his own might and power and lordship in freedom. He discovers himself as the lord of himself, who rules in mastery and governs in sovereign freedom, who takes his own destiny of freedom in his own hands. He discovers himself as the master of his own fate and fortune, the governor of himself and his inner subjectivity. He discovers himself as the possessor of himself. Man, who as freedom stands ready to serve himself, is called by freedom to self-development, self-cultivation, self-culture, self-*expansion,* and thus to the expansion of his own lordship and his own particular domain.

This self-expansion has as its limit or aim the following: that the self becomes at the same time *self*-being and *being,* so as to have the freedom to find itself in its own characteristic being, and remove the last traces of contingency from self-being; to gain complete self-possession in *aseitas,* being from and to and of itself; in brief, to gain *free* freedom instead of contingent freedom.

In fact this amounts to the self's "dis-realization" of its own contingency, and the incorporation of "reality" into the realm of the sovereign self; to the conquest of this reality around us and in us; to the actualization and realization of man's lordship and form-creating power over reality; to the *cultural* duty of man, in which he puts reality at his own service, takes possession of reality, incorporates it, governs it, rules it, makes himself its undisputed master.

This crusade of man is called by Sartre his existential *transcending.* Man transcends being, on the way to his own unlimited self-being; and transcends, in the first place, the being that man himself in a sense is. This transcendence, needless to say, has no connection with a belief in a transcendent God. Transcending is a characteristic and an existential qualification of man and of human activity. It is completely immanent in human freedom and human consciousness, and inseparable from them.

How does this crusade fare, according to Sartre? Man is a lack, an absent totality in a present incompleteness, and as such he must busy himself in filling this lack and thus fulfilling himself. He is a self only in a deficient manner. Though he is freedom and consciousness and nihilating act, he must nevertheless dwell in being, and can thus establish his own foundation and subsequent lordship by virtue of his own factuality and contingency. He is free only on the basis of determinism.

Man's task is thus to rise above and escape from the sovereignty of the absurd. That is his Sisyphus-like task. Behind him he has contingency, which he needs in order to be. Ahead of him he has his self-expansion, the dynamic of self-creation in sovereign self-rule based on nihilation of being. His lordship lies in this, that he is prepared to so far cancel out the contingency of his own factuality that he can then, in sovereign self-government, freely and consciously *accept* this contingency. In this sense he can and he must, he is duty-bound by his own freedom and self-respect, take on and *accept* his own birth and his own existence. Even in the denial of this duty in suicide, he cannot escape the acceptance of his own birth; for he can make plans for suicide only after he has existentially accepted the fact that he "is there." Self-consciousness without the existential act of freedom cannot exist. *Consciousness* of the self's factuality is not mere brute factuality, and is thus different from other factuality. In his consciousness of his own factuality, man encircles and obviates this very factuality; he is then master of himself, and takes *possession* of his own factuality and contingency. Through this consciousness, he comes to *lordship* over his own factual existence, and he rules over his past as *his* conscious past.

This holds true of all of man's past. Since it is past, we no longer have it in our power; it *is*, and is identical with itself. It can no longer be changed or canceled out. But before it can be past, it must be accepted as "past-ness" by us, in the present. If I experience my past as my own, then I must make myself conscious of it. And my freedom lies precisely in this becoming conscious of it. I nihilate it, I make it into "my past," into that which I am not now, and so I place it at a distance from myself. Only after I do that am I prepared freely to take it up and *accept* it as actually being my own past, and to take it along with myself into the future. In this acceptance there is transcendence, and in this transcendence there is nihilation. I, nihilating the past, take it up as a burden upon my shoulders. I exercise *lordship* over it because I take it up freely. I rule it as I bear it. And what does not belong to man's past? Sartre includes in man's past everything that man *is*. And thus, for example, the *body*. For as consciousness, I can make myself distant from the body; and this nihilating act of freedom which affirms that I am *not* my body, is preceded by my body's being. That is, my body already *is*, before my nihilating act of freedom puts my body at a distance from what I *am*. And hence from the standpoint of my consciousness, my body's being is a "past being," and thus a part of my past. So, according to Sartre, it can be said that man in a sense freely accepts his own body, and freely rules over it, since his consciousness freely accepts his bodiliness and his bodily being after first placing it at a distance through the act of nihilation.

And the lordship of man over his own world of being reaches still further, says Sartre. Anything *of which* we can be conscious — with the one exception of the existential notion of self in the pre-reflexive *cogito* — is not itself an act of consciousness, and hence it must be something which is, which belongs to the actuality of being. Well, we can distinguish between joy, desire, pain, sorrow, belief, moods and our *consciousness* of joy, desire, etc. Therefore these also belong to the reality of non-subjective being. Man can isolate himself, by his conscious nihilating act of freedom, from these contents of consciousness, these experiences, these moods. Thus we can say that man, by the distancing function of his free consciousness, can put his own joy, desire, etc. at a distance, so that he is not identical with them. He no longer *is* his joy, desire, etc.; he transcends all of these in his rich psychic diversity; and through this transcendence of joy, desire, etc., he can *accept* that past which he has transcended as being his own past, his own avowed and accepted past. Man, in his existential self-consciousness, is *along side* of his psychic experiences, but in such a manner that he can constantly rise above them, and differentiate his self from them, because of the nihilating action of his existential self-ness.

And so it becomes more and more apparent how great the realm is which is ruled existentially by man's consciousness. He governs his moods, his passions, his experience, and his knowledge; in existential fashion he rules them. The world of the being of all of these things stand ready to serve him, and whether this world of being will remain as being, or whether man will take it with him, as "past," into the future, depends on man's free acceptance or his rejection of it.

It is in this broadening of the lordship of human freedom that Sartre, in my opinion, begins to come dangerously close to picturing man as a schizophrenic might picture him. Is this not man as viewed by a psychopath, whose lust for power goes hand in hand with neurotic anxiety and a persecution complex?

At any rate, Sartre's ideas about the distance between free consciousness and the emotions and experience of this free consciousness reduce human existence to a null-existence. Everything can be stripped away and abstracted from man, without affecting the inner core of man, the free consciousness, the inner act of freedom. So man, and man's consciousness, becomes more clearly merely a "gap in being," a "nothing," a "nihilation." The increasing lordship exercised by the self goes along with the increasing dissection of the self's reality.

This is clarified still further in Sartre's treatment of choice, or, better, of *choosing*. Man *is* that which he *chooses* to be. It is in his power to choose what he will be, to choose his own being. The one basic thing that he need worry about is to make sure that this freedom of choosing is not taken from him. He has the responsibility not so much to choose one thing or another, but to *choose for choosing*. His existential duty is to choose for freedom to choose. Even more could be abstracted in principle from the choice and the chosen, if we wanted, but this is existentially irrelevant.

This *power of choice* which man possesses knows no limits. It reveals to us the power and lordship of sovereign freedom. Man chooses his own past as his own, he chooses his emotions as his own, he chooses his own pain as *his* pain. And likewise he chooses his own body as his own, and even chooses his own birth, by distancing himself from it and then accepting it freely as his. Nothing is outside the competence of this freedom of choice. All of reality is included in man's power of choice, and thus under his unlimited lordship.

For being simply *is*, dumbly, in brute fashion. It is only because of man that being *is there*. There — where? In view of man. That is the only "there" that can be. "There" is a reality, a world, a chaos, only because man in his freedom of choice creates this "there," brings the world in its "being there" into existence. But in the measure that being "is there," it stands unconditionally under the control of the act of freedom which man's self is. This ability to make reality "be there" is the act of mastery which lays the ground for, and makes possible, all further human cultural development of forms and structure. Reality is the domain of man's lordship and power. The Second World War "is there" only if I place it within my view, choose to be conscious of it, and accept it for myself. And thus nothing can happen "there" unless I am responsible for it. Man, like Atlas, carries the burden of all reality on his shoulders. And he possesses, like a God, lordship and rule over all of reality. He rules and possesses everything that is. As lord of himself, he is (in principle) lord of the world. His self-being dominates the world of being. The expansion of the domain of the self finds no limit in the world.

This sovereign freedom and this monopoly of lordship demand, from inner necessity, that no man may count on himself, let alone count on anyone else. Any *continuity* is an attack on the distancing function of freedom, on freedom's power. Freedom means precisely this, to be completely discontinuous. No man may act in good faith, for he then denies his own freedom.

Anyone who calls himself a coward is untrue to his freedom. For he *is* a coward only insofar as he chooses to be a coward. He rules over his cowardice, and he is a coward only by virtue of his permanent and continual choice for that kind of being. Only someone who dies a coward, and thus is bereft of consciousness and freedom, is a coward for all ages, an irrevocable coward. And the same is true of anyone who calls himself a believer; he is also untrue to his freedom. He is a believer only in the measure that he continually chooses to be one. He must choose again and again, continually; choose, after nihilating his past belief, for belief; since belief is something "outside of" and therefore "in contrast to" his own consciousness.

Man rules completely over his own religiousness, his own religious-being. So anyone who calls himself a believer misunderstands himself, and gives up his own sovereign lordship and power.

Sartre combines all these considerations into the position that *there is no human nature*. In other words, the only definition that can be given of man is that he cannot be defined. For man rules over everything that he is, and thus surely also decides whether he will *choose* to be the same tomorrow as he is today. He is — for himself as well as for others — unpredictable, unknowable, unfathomable. His freedom *founds* him, gives him his foundation; a foundation in the abyss of nothingness. Man is in the unreality of Nothing and Annihilation, pure inner-ness and subjectivity.

Still another example might be given to make this clear. I might decide today to give up my career as an actor tomorrow, and I might have strong motives for this decision; but I should not suppose that this will mean anything tomorrow. For I cannot decide today that I will refuse to decide the whole matter afresh tomorrow; I must do precisely that; I am doomed to freedom. Tomorrow I will look at this decision of today as something which is past, which is, which has being, and thus something which I (tomorrow) am *not;* today's decision will be, tomorrow, something which is outside my consciousness, which is an object, which is a thing.

My existential decisions of now become in the next moment a part of the world of being, *of which* I can be conscious, which I can place over against myself, and which thus becomes "loosed" from me (without my consciousness and act of freedom being affected), and which are thus outside me, absolute, part of the world of being. And meanwhile I am loosed from them, absolved of them, in my inner-ness; I have them in my sovereign power, and decide as sovereign about them as something objective, something "other," something alien.

Sartre treats what he calls *situations* in a similar spirit. Man develops himself through being in particular situations. Indeed, his birth is already "situative." His situation includes the "contingent" state of affairs in which the existential self-consciousness and the existential decision find themselves involved. That is, in a "situation" there is an encounter between the existential situations, freely made in pure sovereignty, and the contingent state of affairs in the world of being, the here and now, the *hic and nunc*. I am forty years old, took part in the fighting around Dunkirk, was born in Spain; one parent was a gambler, the other a nervous intellectual; my body is misformed, my emotional life melancholy, my will-power weak, my social position unstable, etc. etc. — all this is a situation. And this situation is not created through any momentary existential decision of mine. It stands before me as an independent and inexplicable obstacle. I "encounter" it, I am "imprisoned" in it, cannot change it, cannot escape it. And, apart from my freedom of consciousness, it would seem that I *am* my situation, am identical with it: I am forty years old, the son of a gambler, etc.

But we are forgetting one thing. For, because I am my own existential act of freedom, "am" existentially, I am not identical with my situation. Indeed, the roles are now reversed; "There" could be no "situation" if I was not an existential center of freedom. That the situation "is there" is due to my act of freedom. And thus it can better be said that I call my situation into being, rather than that my situation limits me. I implicate myself freely and independently in the situations in which I develop. I give myself to the situation voluntarily, I engage myself in the situation, *engager*. I do this by accepting the situation as mine, freely and consciously. I rise above the situation in the existential act by which I make myself distant from it and thus loose myself from it. And therefore I *govern* my situation, because I cannot implicate myself in it without first loosing myself from it (*engager* presupposes *dégager*), without first choosing my situation, choosing to accept it. Man is *situationsmächtig*, he dominates his situation, because of his unconditional, unlimited and absolute freedom. In this sense, the situation in which I find myself is one which I have created; its "burden" would not be a burden if I did not voluntarily take it on my shoulders, through the power of my nihilating transcendence. The alien and arbitrary obstacle of the situation has now been conquered, by myself and through myself; it now belongs to the domain and lordship of my existential freedom; it has been incorporated into my realm. It thus raised no insurmountable obstacle to the expansion of my power.

In my ontological experience of anxiety, I discover that the situation is not the master, but that I am in principle master of the situation, and responsible for my lordship over it, and so also responsible for my situation in all its extent. My situation is constantly chosen by me, it stands under me, I possess it, through the power of my existential freedom.

And there are still further implications to this line of thought.

The individual finds other individuals next to and in contrast to himself. The existential structuring of reality, its "is there"-ness, means not only that reality is related to *my* perspective, but also that it is related to "the other" individual's perspective. And this is so completely true that reality's characteristic "is there"-ness, its being viewed by someone else, its *être-pour-autri*, holds also for each individual. The individual, too, is *être-pour-autri*, being viewed by another. And Sartre makes this something which is inseparable from man's existence, something given, a datum; it belongs to the ontological and existential structure of man's human "being."

This means that any other individual can direct his consciousness towards me, or his nihilating act of freedom, and thereby include me in his domain, make me subject to his inner consciousness. And my *être-pour-autri* is an original, an ontological thing; I cannot escape from it, even in my consciousness. There is thus always the possibility that the other individual will incorporate what "I am," all of my "being," in his "world." His "situation" may include me, and his ability to transcend his situation means that he can transcend my being, and imprison it in his domain. And even if this perchance does not actually happen, there is always the possibility that it may happen at any moment. To the extent that I am not wholly conscious of an inner act of will, I am in principle exposed in my nakedness to this sovereign and humiliating act of "the other"; I am exposed to the other, I am *être-pour-autri*.

Sartre develops this notion further in his treatment of the *glance,* the covertous eye which the other casts upon me (or at least can do so). His glance dispossesses me, and takes for himself everything he can see of me. This concept is erotically tinged, in Sartre. The glance of the other strips me, denudes me, takes away my privacy and intimacy, and violates the sovereignty which I as an act of freedom possess over everything around me and in me. In the experience of shame, I realize that I can be objectivized by the other, objectivized by him into a mere being, a part of reality, robbed of my consciousness and act of freedom, and in any event robbed of the subjectivity of my act of freedom. The glance of another, by which he transcends everything that "is" mine, and brings it under his control, enslaves me and includes me in the domain of *his* lordship of freedom. "Someone is watching me"; that is the opposite of my freedom's lordship.

But there is another side to this. I can put a stop to this "theft of self" by transcending the other; by casting *my* glance on him, my glance on his glance. I can then transcend his transcending, and overcome his power over me, and his power over himself. I can dispossess the dispossesser. But — why cannot he in his turn transcend my dispossession of him? As an existential center of freedom, he cannot let this dispossession go unchallenged.

This all means, then, that the "world," including the world within myself, is a battlefield, on which the continual struggle between myself and everyone else is fought out. It is a struggle for unending mastery over this world. Every conquest I make (through the power of my freedom and consciousness), whether of reality round about me or reality within myself, is a threatened conquest and an insecure conquest. Each new act of freedom is a conquest and a dispossession of my competing dispossessers. I and everyone elses live in a "social" relationship which is nothing else than a conflict, a conflict in which the individual who last transcends in the one who triumphs, that is, the individual who lives the longest. I can make my lordliness of freedom evident even in my last glance, which I can use to transcend another. His confiscation finds in my confiscation an unending boundary-violation; his in mine and mine in his, each forfeiting and transcending in turn. The conflict is one which never ends, and peace is unattainable; but defeat is just as indefinite as victory, for the act of freedom can never really be stolen or reduced to a thing; my glance is always a ruler's glance.

Closely related to this lordship over all the reality around me and within me, including the lordship over the reality, the being of the other, is my *responsibility*.

According to Sartre, this responsibility extends just as far as our freedom and power. Since I can choose whether or not to freely accept a toothache, I am responsible for the toothache's reality, it "is there" because of my freedom, I am responsible for all of reality. That the Second World War "is there" is my fault. It could only "be there" because of my choice to accept it in the present as a past war.

This expansion of responsibility to include everything, which makes every man an Atlas, bearing the whole world on his shoulders, actually can lead to nothing else than the complete undermining of all true responsibility. *Qui trop embrasse, mal étreint:* he who embraces something too much crushes it to death. The results of Sartre's mania for responsibility are just that.

His idea that responsibility can exist only on a basis of sovereign freedom is pure humanism. Personal responsibility, says Sartre, demands personal freedom. Sartre claims (rightly) in his defense of his philosophy, *L'Existentialism est un humanisme,* that he and he alone is truly humanistic, and this because he radicalizes the sovereignty of freedom and the autonomy of freedom. And he warns his opponents — from a humanistic point of view, rightly — that they discharge man from the seriousness of his responsibility in the measure that they damage the unlimitedness of man's sovereign freedom.

These are not simply technical philosophical questions which are at issue here; we are concerned with the most basic problems, religious problems. When Sartre explains the fear of God as an illicit abdication of man's freedom and responsibility, an abdication of man's lordship, a radical enslaving of man, he does, to be sure, give full honor to his dogma of freedom. But at the same time he makes clear that this idea of pure sovereign freedom and responsibility is not only a-Christian but also anti-Christian and anti-theistic. The splendor of Sartrian man is stolen splendor, a tarnishing (an attempt at tarnishing) the splendor of almighty God.

Can Sartre's idea of the "self-responsibility" of man really be called *responsibility?* Can the monologue of freedom really give a response to the dialogue of responsibility (which means, literally, owing an answer)? That man is a "law unto himself" is an idea which is religiously just as illicit and apostate an idea as that God is a law unto himself. Responsibility demands a freedom which is subject to order, bound to order, placed under authority. It demands a theonomy, not an autonomy: it does not irreligiously throw man into the arms of an arbitrariness deified into law, into the power of an irresponsible freedom which incorporates all law and norm and value in itself; responsibility does not throw man into the dictatorship of anarchy.

But that is what Sartre does. For the greater glory and power of existential freedom, he incorporates all of actuality into the realm of the "is there" of man's freedom's imperialism. The chaotic reality of being receives from this "being there" its first and basic ordering. Thus it becomes a *cosmos;* it becomes completely *humanized.* Man can recognize his own product and structuring in everything he encounters in that reality of "being there"; so complete is the meaning-giving power of man's conscious act of freedom. The "world" as cosmos belongs to the domain of self-ness, *the circuit de l'ipséité;* it is a field which man enters and puts under cultivation, brings to culture, as man journeys towards his own divine self (the *en-soi-pour-soi*). This "world," this chaos become cosmos, is no longer different from what Fichte's absolute idealism would call "nature"; its obstacles have become exercises for our duty to freedom, obstacles which serve to help bring man to his final aim — to constitute himself as self-founding being, as "God," and so supersede his present self, which is an incomplete whole, a partial god, *Dieu manqué,*

Man's mighty freedom not only produces a cosmos, in which the chaos of being has been structured by self-creating man, but also creates norms and values. These too are under the lordship of man. Sartre bitterly opposes the idea that values (he uses "values" to mean objective norms, as do all subjectivists) exist independently of man, "written in the heavens"; they would then hamper man's freedom. He passionately execrates the Enlightenment for not having abolished God completely, and for continuining to speak of objective values and norms which do not find their orgin in man's sovereign freedom. Sartre sees himself as a true apostle of humanism when he makes a clean sweep of all this residue of an outdated belief in a deistic God. Values are nothing more than goals, aims, which man freely sets for himself; one of the means he creates to help him in his struggle to reach his final objective, self-deification. Every ordinance, every norm, every law is relative; they are dependent on the expansion of man's freedom; they are means which man creates only to transcend; and thus means which must be thrown off and transcended. Values exist in order to disappear. There is nothing absolute, nothing holy, except man's freedom and its expansion. And this expansion of freedom's realm must be *dynamic*. The consolidation of an established power of freedom is not absolute; for as *established*, it belongs to the past, it falls into the "being" of reality, and thus becomes an obstacle which must be overcome. The essential "value," then, is unreachable: it is that which man lacks, and tries to reach in order to become "God." It lies on the other side of reality, even on the other side of the actualization of man's power. It calls man to rise above himself; it causes his standing before what he could be, and thus his always being "behind himself." It gives an unending character to the extension of his power. His task is a Sisyphus-like task, the filling of a bottomless container.

On the other hand, man's task is what gives him glory; gives him the assurance that he is always more than he is; indeed, that he is not (now) what he is (when complete), and that he is what he is not. Thus man is his own value, his own norm. Man's existence is self-creating, and in his self-founding he is also the creator of every norm and value.

In this way Sartre humanizes norms and values, and saves man's sovereignty from the grave of an anti-human heteronomy. He has incorporated norms and values into man's power and lordship, and thus heightened the glory of man. Man becomes the arbiter of his own destiny, forming his own ideals and creating his own norms. His consciousness of norms is his consciousness of himself, thus; his self-consciousness is his freedom; his freedom is his sovereignty. His self-culture is norm-creating and norm-destroying, so that no power can rise against man, not even his own "creation." Man is responsible, as we have seen, for his own freedom, the freedom for freedom, the choice to choose. And in the same measure, he is responsible for choosing revolution against the established, and the destruction that causes; for preventing all institutional stability, positive law, historical tradition; for opposition against the dominating rule of a continuous and evolving culture. Man thus is the crisis of all "existing" culture, so that he can remain the sovereign lord of his own self-culture. His *nihilating* power is the key to his unlimited self-creating lordship of freedom, the impregnable castle of his feudal domain. It makes him the lord and master of the whole of reality, not excluding the realm of values and law.

The self-worship of man, or man's auto-eroticism if you prefer, is completely unlimited in Sartre's thought. And it could hardly be otherwise when the sovereignty of human freedom is so completely radicalized.

IV. THE CHECK TO FREEDOM'S LORDSHIP

It is evident from the foregoing that the lordship exercised by freedom is precarious, perilous, fragile. It is threatened from all sides, and in danger at all times.

This is not true of the act of freedom itself. As a subjective and inner act, it is enclosed by the Annihilation of Nothingness. It is true that its factuality, its "being," is contingent; but we have seen that contingency does not imply that there is any danger of disappearance; contingency *is*, and thus is eternal. The act of freedom is outside of and beyond any temporalizing, since temporalizing first becomes possible after the act of nihilation, and that act is the basis for the *act* of freedom, not for the factuality of freedom.

The *act* of freedom, as subjective act, is impregnable. Only death puts an end to it. And it is not at all haunted by the fear of death; a philosophy of death such as Heidegger's is foreign to Sartre. You can take away all my power, but the subjectivity of the act of freedom and the *project* of expanding the power of freedom is impregnable, thanks to the inconquerable castle of nihilation. Wherever there is consciousness, this act of freedom and its project of self-development is safe and sound. Any particular choice I make may be threatened. but the choice to choose is subjective and cannot be threatened. A prisoner can be just as conscious of this inviolable freedom as anyone else, says Sartre; indeed, perhaps better conscious, because he is a prisoner. In a sense his freedom is greater than that of his guard. For the prisoner can do that which his jailor cannot do, make plans to escape; and no jailor can take away this transcending of his freedom. Otherwise it would be a poor and scanty (or empty and rotten) self-sufficiency.

But it is completely different when we concern ourselves with the power of freedom over our own surroundings, over the "situation" of our own body and its past. Freedom's power then is fragile, it is always at stake, it can always be undermined; it is essentially (as the power of temporalization) *finite* and finite-izing. From one moment to the next, it is continually exposed in its nakedness to the power of brute being, to the absurd, to chaos, to reality.

The floodtide of brute being washes over the whole domain of the lordship of freedom. Freedom must be continually fought for. Its *establishing* means its downfall. Established freedom is an impossibility, for the established is as such already part of the past, as is everything which is not the act of freedom or incorporated in it. Even the "nothingness" of all things outside the act of freedom "has been," is past. *Le néant est... été*, says Sartre in intentionally inharmonious French; and by this he means that consciousness and freedom and subjectivity cannot establish themselves, for once they "are," they already have been; and once they have been, they are past, and are no longer part of the existential act, and no longer have any real existential being. They must therefore be continually created anew. Just as the tangent to a circle can remain a tangent only so long as the tangent-point is *not* included in the circle, so freedom can keep its rule over reality only so long as the rule does not become "real" and does not become part of the realm of "being."

The *en-soi*, being, continually forces its own independence and absurd contingency on the power of freedom; because it endures, it can continually break away from the lordship of consciousness. Man's cultural humanizing of reality, bound as it is to the actualization of a momentary act of freedom, becomes in the next instant annihilated and incorporated in the "meaningless" reality of being. The *pour-soi*-consciousness, the existence of man, is constantly driven back by the *en-soi;* man's nihilating power is constantly engulfed by being; culture by petrification; expansion by consolidation. There can be no thought of a lasting result of man's cultural activity, for the *application* of freedom's rules lies outside the subjectivity of the act of freedom, and thus, as "applied," it belongs to the realm of being. It is; and when it is, it belongs to the past. It is an object, visible, loosed from the creative sovereignty of man, and hence an *obstacle* to the next temporalization of the self. The applications and results of each human project are a hindrance to the next project. Tradition, that which the German idealists called objectivized spirit, *den objectiven Geist,* is viewed by the existentialism of finiteness as an opponent of man's true existence, something which is brute "being." Culture as *formed* culture is a continual threat to, and dispossession of, the power of existential existence. An abyss separates the lordly form-*creation* of man and the resultant fixed form; an abyss which in principle is like the abyss between Nothing and Being. Hence all cultural activity is a Sisyphus-like task. The form-giving power of man's sovereign act of freedom is stolen and petrified by contingent being. The rule of freedom as shown in its structuring of self and of being is immediately pushed back and destroyed by the superior power of being. The actualization of the act of freedom and its culture-creating project immediately falls outside the rule of freedom, and stands as an obstacle in the path of freedom.

So, then, the value of all this transcending of self and of being, of this self-creation, *se faire,* and the humanization of being, lies only in its intensity. For the results of freedom are, as results, a check to the power of freedom. Culture is, as structured and established culture, the *crisis* of man's sovereign form-creation, an attack on man, an inducement to self-alienation, a seduction to self-betrayal.

And since, for Sartre, man's subjectivity can never rise above Nothingness, and is based on nihilation, and man's transcendence is based on the actualization of nothingness — how could it be otherwise? The obstacles are, in contrast to freedom, eternal; being itself is an obstacle, and more than an obstacle, for it is contingent and absurd. Since being "is," and man's subjectivity is "nothing," being is a more powerful pole than the pole of freedom, so far as man's "being" is concerned. The materialism of Sartre is "ontologically" stronger than his idealism of freedom, just as his idealism of freedom is more valuable than his materialism. Man's existence, his true existence, "is" not, does not have "being." In a sense, man's (true) existence does not exist. Mounnier, as mentioned above, has this in mind when he speaks of Sartre's *in*-existentialism.

Hence man's consciousness (and his subjectivity and his act of freedom, for all three are synonymous) is a conquerer of being, a gap in being, an emptying of being, a *décompressie* of being, the empty in the full, a relation which has no being, a relation of nullity. Therefore contingent being is always able to recover its dominance over human existence and its power. Man's check, that which checks man, is his history. Man's rule and lordship can in many instances go no further than *acceptance;* acceptance of the *burden* of existence, acceptance of the "given" situation, acceptance of his own body, acceptance of his own past, acceptance of the situation of conflict which we call society. This acceptance may mean unlimited sovereignty, but I can have no other body than my own, no other situation than the given, no other past except that which is mine by chance, no other society than that in which I find myself — even if these are all freely given to myself by myself. The power of being's contingent factuality breaks away, threatening me, from the rule of my sovereign lordship. Body, situation, past, society — these do not give up their contingency, even if I want them to. They are explosions of absurdity, and not due to any subjective act of man.

But actually, are these really explosions of absurdity? Is not Sartre's contempt for anything which does not subject itself to man the cause for the nausea aroused in him by the experience of being? When Sartre writes that it is absurd that my mother should be my mother (for I might just as well — it would be no more absurd — be her father), then we ask ourselves in some amazement why Sartre never even considers the possibility that he himself is absurd when he talks this way. The chief character in Sartre's *La Naussée*, Roquaintain, says that a stone is absurd, but that he himself is surely not. But such a fantastic assertion is nothing more then fantasy. Indeed, less than fantasy; abnormal. For only abnormality can delight in making the normal abnormal and the abnormal normal.

Sartre, in his *L'Être et le Néant*, wished to give a philosophical justification for this abnormal position. With undeniable acuteness, he bases this justification on a system which stresses the sovereign free self, and the contingent being of actuality; and in the course of this justification he strips reality of its value, and denies the God of reality, by placing reality *(since* it lies outside man's power!) in the realm of absurdity. A Christian can only be disgusted with Sartre's disgust with reality, and be again convinced that the wisdom of this world is foolishness in the eyes of God.

The overwhelming power of this being (absurd though it may be) becomes crystal-clear when we note how Sartre does not hesitate to identify man with his situation, his past, his body — indeed, to identify man with those things he can be conscious of. Then Sartre writes this way: man *is* his body, and nothing more; he *is* his situation; he *is* his past, his belief, etc.; he is *la chose*, a thing, the thing (which he perceives). He is so closely related to the things he perceives that he *is* them. He is separated from them by a boundary, but the boundary is not real. The boundary is that of un-real dis-realization. It seems to me that in Sartre's treatment of absurdity there is plenty of data for anyone who wants to make a study of real absurdity!

This identification with being is indeed the opposite of man's sovereign lordship over his own past, his own body, his situation, over all of reality and all "things." This identification is the continual *check* of man's lordship. And thus Sartre takes back with one hand the freedom he had given man with the other.

Sartre sees all society and all social relationships, all public life and public rules, as paradoxical; not merely in the sense of an "impossible possibility," but in the sense of pure impossibility. To live socially is essentially impossible, for other individuals can do nothing else than struggle to develop their freedom's lordship over themselves and over all of reality — and thus over my reality. It is impossible that things could be otherwise. So our vaunted "society" is actually only a series of encounters, encounters involving rivalry, struggle, dispossessing of the other without friendship or love, without real relationship.

Social life in any meaningful sense is impossible; what there is is simply a series of encounters. And these are encounters which we must use to conquer the other individual, to subjugate him, dominate him, take away from him his mastery of the situation. Transcending the other involves humiliating the other; the first glance is already humiliating, and produces shame in the other.

The destructive results of such an outlook are easily apparent. Since auto-eroticism and auto-sexuality plays such an important role in Sartre's thought, it is to be expected that he would devote much time both in his plays and in his main philosophical work, to marriage; to love and desire in and outside of marriage. This treatment works to the detriment of marriage, as might be expected, but it also tends to stress how *any* erotic relationship between individuals, irrespective of sex, must result in a check to freedom. Sometimes such relationships preclude the freedom to nihilate one's self; then again they may preclude the freedom to nihilate the other. Sometimes they preclude the freedom to dispossess the other; or, again, they may preclude the freedom to allow the dispossessing of one's self by the other.

There are two main themes in the background of all Sartre's teaching on social relations, inter-human bonds and intercourse. First, the lordship of freedom possessed both by myself and by the other; and, second, the check to the freedom of myself and the other. This last is a favorite theme of Sartre's: "My neighbor is hell."

Can the inherent check to this extreme individualistic existentialism be more strongly shown than in that conclusion, to which Sartre is driven by inner necessity? Neither humanism nor Christianity will find here any remnants of love for one's neighbor, let alone love for God, which lies far beyond the horizon of this existentialist thinker.

Sartre's "preaching" about the inherent check to this individualistic lordship of freedom strengthens us in our conviction that love is the fulfilling of the *law;* and that Sartre's dogma of freedom is the counter-"gospel"(!) to the gospel of love as the fulfilling of the law. To anyone who has any appreciation of the Christian law and gospel, Sartre's teaching on the check to freedom's lordship, and the neighbor as hell, is an evidence of the truth and reality of God's rule: the rule of God who does not allow the basic law of love to God and one's neighbor to be denied or profaned. Sartre's denial of this basic law produces the darkness without a dawn in which he wanders; the night of the neighbor as hell, and myself as my neighbor's hell. We can thus take Sartre as seriously as he takes himself, but from a different angle of vision; we can take him more seriously, as being personally serious. He cannot be irritated at us for this; it is according to his own teaching.

V. THE DIALECTIC OF LORDSHIP AND FAILURE

Sartre's idealism of freedom could hardly be called existentialism if he limited himself simply to absolute subjective freedom, which as such knew no limits. And it would not be existentialism if he viewed the inner act of freedom as the source of all reality, as Fichte did.

Nor would it be existentialism if he explained and deduced man's freedom from the contingent world of being. Bochenski does not do justice to Sartre when he characterizes his thought simply as epiphenomenal materialism, in which spirit and consciousness and the act of freedom are simply epiphenomena, auxiliary phenomena, of material being.

Sartre is neither a pure idealist of freedom nor a pure materialist.

In neither case would there be a place for Sartre's existentialism. His existential philosophy is characterized rather by his stress on the existential relationship which binds together his opposing emphases: the existential relationship between freedom and objective being, between *neant* and *être*, between freedom and contingency, between anxiety and nausea, between *engager* and *degager*, between eternity and temporalizing, between unlimited freedom and limited choice, between chaos and cosmos, between man and the world, between subjective and objective, between subjectivizing and objectivizing, between immanence and transcendence, between ruling and accepting, between creation and burden-bearing, between consciousness and being, spirit and body, *pour-soi* and *en-soi*, glory and doom, meaning and absurdity, duty and uselessness, lordship and failure, the potency of freedom and the impotency of being, self-acceptance and *conscience malheureuse*, deifying and demonizing, self-possession and self-alienation, becoming and being, responsibility and event, domination and enslavement, being and "being there," factual necessity and spontaniety, self-alienation and self-establishment.

The lordship of freedom is counterbalanced by the check to freedom. And if we do not keep these pairs of concepts clearly in mind — the first *and* the second, the first *in contrast to* the second — we will miss the essence of Sartre's philosophy. It is precisely this dialectic, this polar relationship between motifs, which is basic to Sartre's existentialism.

Sometimes the emphasis and orientation may lie in nausea, being matter (as in *La Naussée*); sometimes in freedom and the act of freedom (as in *l'Existentialism est un Humanisme*); but this does not affect the fact that Sartre needs and keeps both poles, and must do so if he is to be an existentialist. It is the dialectic of being and becoming, contingency and freedom, etc. etc., the unstable balance between them which is characteristic and basic in Sartre's philosophy. Thus in the choice, in which freedom's nihilating power "encounters" being, freedom subjects being to its own power and lordliness; but the reverse is also true; by the choice, freedom is ended, and being subjects freedom to its power, and dooms freedom to be continually checked. Factuality always escapes freedom's power; but freedom always escapes factuality's power. There is no reconciliation, no higher synthesis. Sartre rejects (as did Kierkegaard) Hegel's idea of reconciliation of opposites in a higher synthesis. The eschatology of Sartre, his view of the "last things," can therefore not be presented as a view of a unity. The "end" is of a dual nature.

First, we might ask what becomes of freedom's struggle for lordship, which aims at the self-founding of freedom as its own foundation of being, as the "unity" of *en-soi-pour-soi*, by which freedom could transcend contingency by becoming true freedom instead of contingent freedom. Well, this aim ends in an illusion, in the incomplete god, the *Dieu manque;* its only meaning is uselessness, its ideal is unattainable, its actualization impossible. The "glory" of man rests in the pursuit of an illusion and a search for the unattainable. As he hunts down this illusion of self-founding (alias self-deification), he creates through his nihilation of being a lordship and power; but this lordship is fragile and always threatened, and it ends in nothingness. From nihilation to illusion: that is the first vista offered by existentialism.

And the second vista is offered when we consider that role played by contingency,that obstacle to man which is being. One thing which man can never incorporate in his realm of lordship and power is death. And death, a "brute fact," finally destroys the original act of freedom completely so that nothing remains, and what was a "man" — a dialectic unity of consciousness and being, freedom and contingency — becomes merely being, contingency, "matter." With death, the darkness of the contingent and absurd rolls over the last light of freedom and meaning. "Man" returns to full, eternal being; his temporalizing consciousness is gone forever; the "gap in being" is finally closed.

Ontologically speaking, Sartre gives a primary place to being. Consciousness exists along side of being, not vice versa. Consciousness "is" not (or is "not"), while being "is." Consciousness is an emptying of being, a degradation of being, a gap in being. On the other hand, however, consciousness is never more than an "ideal" and unreal distance away from being; it is a nihilation of being, an aversion to being, a transcending of being, but it can never shake itself loose from being. Being is, whether there is consciousness or not; consciousness is present only where there is being, and cannot exist without being. Being is *en-soi,* self-contained, while consciousness can only be immanent in itself by existing along side of being and reality, existing, in a sense, outside itself. Being never becomes consciousness or adopts a conscious mode of existence; but the reverse is not true. In a sense, man *is* the things that he perceives; but the reverse is not true. And everything which has been said about consciousness holds also for man's act of freedom, for the two are the same. In some places Sartre seems to say that the act of freedom itself originates in being, "as if" being wanted to become conscious of itself, "as if" being wanted to stand in internal relation to itself, "as if" being wanted to found itself and transcend itself. But elsewhere he makes it clear that the origin of freedom in, and out of, primary contingency is a self-founding originality; that is, that freedom cannot really be explained in terms of contingency; the "as if" explanation is a pseudo-explanation. The one pole, man's freedom, cannot be deduced from its opposite pole, that of contingent being. But, says Sartre, even granting this self-reliance and independence of consciousness and the act of freedom over against being, it still remains true that the originality of the act of freedom is itself contingent and absurd. Its origin, its originality is not a *free* originality, but only the origin or originality *of* freedom.

The tidal character, the overwhelming character of being, is brought to pregnant expression in Sartre's inclusion of everything that does not have consciousness and freedom, in the realm of being; and in the way that being forces freedom and consciousness to nihilation and dis-realization, towards their "presence" in being, towards the inevitable check to freedom. But yet, in typical dialectical fashion, the act of freedom, impregnable within its contingent origin, regains its power and rights in its turn. For, to begin with, there is no possible way in which the inner act of freedom can be objectivized and transformed into being; and, secondly, the origin of freedom is an *événement absolu,* an event inexplicable in terms of contingent being, and as such a wholly "alien" happening in the world of being. Sartre often refers to this as the *surgissement original,* the surging forth of consciousness, completely unexpected by the world of being, and astonishing to it. And, in the third place, the whole of the reality of contingent being can be so completely incorporated in the realm of freedom's lordship that Sartre can say man is "responsible" for his own birth. It should be noted, however, that death cannot be so incorporated; for Sartre (in opposition to Heidegger), death comes from "beyond" and overcomes consciousness. Its absurdity cannot for a moment be humanized or historicized.

In this dialectic between freedom and contingency, limited by the opposing poles of freedom and contingency, each dominating and enclosing the other, contingency has an ontological superiority, a superiority in *being;* but freedom has a superior *value.*

Contingency is valueless, meaningless, aversion-waking, chaotic, unintelligible, irrational, absurd, undifferentiated, objective, scientifically analyzable, revealed. The act of freedom (which man *is)* is value-creating, meaning-giving, responsible, valuable, creating cosmos and order, light, reason, intelligible, differentiated, subjective, inner, hidden.

Sartre's axiological preference for "nothingness" is all its variations (as over against being) is completely understandable. For Nothingness and Freedom and Consciousness are the essentially human. With man, Nothingness comes into the world, and with Nothingness, man. Sartre values man, man in the world, and thus the world; but not the world without man. So even his admission of the superiority in *being* which the objective contingent world possesses is tinged with an axiological coloring, or, if you prefer, an existential — anthropological coloring. He speaks of man, man who is in danger of being crushed by the non-human. Thus, in *La Naussée*, he pictures man's experience of being as the experience of a huge beast of prey who charges against man. Contingency overwhelms man. The superiority of being means the weakness of man as man. The totality of man is the tension-filled unity of consciousness and being, spirit and body; and the "being" if consciousness and spirit is identical with man's bodily character, his contingency. And yet, Sartre does not evaluate man from a materialistic standpoint, in terms of his body; he takes his point of departure in consciousness, in the inner act of freedom; and thus he sees man as a struggle, freedom's struggle to transcend its bodily character, to nihilate its own contingency, and to found itself as free freedom. The essence of man is the struggle of man, the struggle of the act of freedom which man *is*, against contingency; the history of man as a consciously chosen project of destroying being and constituting himself by himself, this self-development, this *se faire* of man, which controls and humanizes his own bodily contingency by making it subject to his self, part of the *circuit de l'ipséité* — this history of man, says Sartre, is the essence of man; this history of the existential struggle, the struggle to subjectivize the contingent, for the greater power and lordliness of man. Man's existence is a struggle, a *luctor et emergo*. The expansion of freedom is followed closely by the check to freedom; but the expansion is not halted, and freedom holds fast against any checkmate; it does this even though it knows its struggle is ultimately useless; no, *because* it knows its struggle is ultimately useless.

The existential, axiological superiority of freedom's struggle to the tidal powers of being is shown further in this, that Sartre does not describe the expansion of freedom as a continual check to the power of being, but rather describes being as a check to the expansion of freedom.

So Sartre's existential anthropology overshadows his materialistic idea of being. Man *is* his body, true enough, in a sense. But this apparently materialistic idea loses this appearance when we consider three things. First, Sartre does not say the reverse (i.e., that man's body is man); second, Sartre says that man is his body only in the sense that he is not his body (i.e., that he is his body in order to transcend it); and third, Sartre teaches that man does not *have* to be his body; he has to be *himself* (i.e., as *Dieu manqué*, an incomplete god, he must seek his true self, which will mean freedom from bodily contingency).

The characteristic existential motif can thus be described also in slightly different terms from those used above; described as the ideal of the subjectivizing of all contingency, the drama of man's struggle to reach this completion, the history of man's useless attempt to actualize this ideal. This drama, this history, is called existence, *Existence*. It implies the dialectic between the humanizing produced by the expansion of freedom, and the check given to this humanizing by the tidal character of being.

Man's existence is hence nothing else than this subjective and *absolute* act of freedom. Existence includes, besides this inner act of freedom, the encounter of freedom with contingent being, which opposes it as an obstacle on the way to self-culture, self-development, and as an obstacle of freedom's control of being. The real existential theme of Sartre's philosophy is the history of this "encounter," written from the viewpoint of the ontological-existential "experience" of this encounter, the experience of anxiety and of nausea. The *tension* involved in this history is caused by the "ontological" impossibility of decisively ending this encounter (and thus man must, if true to himself, choose again and again for a particular encounter), and because it is "ontologically" impossible to use this encounter to establish the almighty power of freedom. Contingency does not allow itself to be destroyed; the attempt fails.

The two facets of this tension can be seen clearly in Sartre's treatment of "situation." This term is equivocal — and for that reason particularly useful for Sartre's existentialism. The same is true of Sartre's use of the term "body"; it is equivocal, and therefore especially useful.

What does Sartre mean by "situation"? The situation is the being that I (in a sense) am, here and now, *ici et ceci*. I am not the whole of reality, for my being is an individual being. And my individual being, combined with my individual environment, is "my situation." My being is a particular concrete past; a historian can study it. I am doomed in my freedom of choice to encounter this individual past, this individual being, and either reject it (through suicide) or accept it by accepting the burden of life, accepting myself-as-my-past.

Along with this choice of my concrete individual situation in time, there arises the choice of accepting my situation in place. Living in the

United States, I freely choose to accept living here. But I am so far limited to the United States that I do not have the freedom of choice to decide to dwell in Australia the next moment. This factual situation is a necessity, a *necessité de fait*.

My freedom of choice exists concretely in an *engager*, a giving of myself to the situation in which I find myself, a volutary involvement. My infinite and unlimited subjective act of freedom remains unlimited so long as I retain my freedom to *choose*. But this same freedom is limited and finite so far as the actual *choice* is concerned, for this is always limited by the situation, bound by *ceci et ici*, by time and place. In my concrete choice, I can effectually do nothing else than to involve myself in the *given* situation. As a given, it falls outside the scope of my creative sovereignty. The extension of my power of freedom to include the situation can be gained only at the cost of "finite-izing" and limiting my unlimited possibilities of freedom by means of a specific choice.

Thus, in choosing to accept situations, sovereign freedom is dominant; but in the concrete *choice* of a particular situation, being gains the upper hand and has its revenge. The "situation" thus includes two aspects, the "free" choosing and the "given" choice; and thus the idea of "situation" is equivocal. Seen from the viewpoint of free *choosing*, the situation in which I find myself is mine, since I implicate myself in it in full existential freedom. First I free myself from it by distancing it from me through nihilation; my *degager* precedes my *engager*, my involvement in the particular situation; my nihilation of the situation, my self-isolation from it, precedes my particular choice and my involvement in a particular situation. In that sense, the situation is mine, and I am master of the situation.

But seen from the viewpoint of the concrete choice, the "situation" presents a totally different appearance. Then it has a double contingency. In the first place, the situation is in no sense an inner act of freedom; it is "being," eternal being, factuality, meaningless. It is what it is, without foundation and without meaning. I do not dominate it, but it dominates me. I can do nothing else than choose it. I am so bound by being that I cannot exist without being in some situation; the act of freedom is a "gap in being," and "lives" in being, and thus must exist in a situation. In order to exist, it must be bound to finiteness.

Furthermore, the specific and concrete particulars of a situation are also a "given," and as such a contingent obstacle to the power of freedom. I can do nothing else than accept this particular situation, this particular past with which I am associated, this toothache, this

Second World War, these particular circumstances. Even if I commit suicide, I do not escape from choosing this particular situation; for when I am dead, I am *wholly* identical with my past, and thus with the *hic et nunc*, the here and now, in which I committed suicide. The "situation," then, is at the same time a check to freedom and a check to contingency, and its unity in the *tension* between the two, a tension which cannot be abolished or sublimated.

Well, what is true about the "situation" — its equivocality, its double sense, and the unity of the hidden tension, is true of the other Sartrian pairs of motifs. We could develop the same things in Sartre's idea of "the body," "the world," *en-soi-pour-soi*, "self-contained being," and so forth.

The existential philosophy consists of an equivocal use of these basic motifs. Thus it teaches, and must teach, both the power and lordship of man, and the check to man; the drama and the tragedy of man's "history." Man is, ontologically speaking, a denied unity, a potential unity (but an impossible unity) of consciousness, freedom, and being; and contingency.

Man is the tension-filled *history* of the fruitless attempt to break through to this impossible unity, to found himself as free freedom, and to incorporate all being in his world, where every trace of contingency will be removed. And if Sartre is to teach the dialectic of lordship and check *(échec)* as the basic truth about man, the framework of this existential anthropology could be nothing else. Man, nearly destroyed by being; and being, nearly destroyed by man. The unending struggle, the glory of man; the finite obstacle, the check to man. Existence as the encounter of this unending struggle, and hence of power-expansion and check. Man, between nihilation and illusion. Culture built through the continual self-constitution of man, through nihilation and illusion, through the loneliness of self-centered exile, through complete self-concern. Man, his own prisoner in his self-isolation, an emptiness casting no shadow, duty-bound to follow an illusion. Man, a half-breed, a cross between pure contingency and pure freedom, half contingent freedom and half free contingency, as much being-destroying as being-actualizing, laboring under the sickness of an unhappy consciousness, a *mauvais conscience*; laboring under permanent and fruitless unrest, driven by this *continuous* drive onwards along his useless way.

VI. EXPOSURE AND UNMASKING

One postulate of Sartre's philosophy is that every man undergoes the infallible ontological experiences of anxiety and nausea. Thanks to these experiential revelations, the two basic structures of our human being, freedom and contingency, are knowable for us and known by us. The experience of anxiety is intimately related to our conscious free being, and reveals to us our nihilating act of freedom. And because of the absurdity of our contingent being, every man experiences the nausea which reveals this to us.

Each of these experiences supports the other. In the experience of nausea, I experience: I am not *that*, I am rather my own not-being and nihilating freedom. And with the experience of anxiety, I experience: my distance from all that merely is and is not free, and the fact and duty of transcending everything that merely is; and thus I indirectly experience being.

Sartre manipulates this postulate of the two ontological experiences to expose and unmask the man of everyday life, the average man, the man who judges himself to be normal, the bourgeois man. For the average man, alas, does not allow himself to be led by the light of these two ontological experiences. He is thus untrue to his own existence, to the dialectial tension between "self" and "being," and he lives in bad faith, *de mauvaise foi*, in unfaithfulness to himself.

Now, if it is true that man's existence is actually the dramatic history of his revolt against the contingency of being, then it is true that man can live an *authentic* life only if he draws the one correct conclusion from these ontological experiences, from his conscious self-presentation of his own freedom and from his nausea for the strongly-sensed absurdity of the whole world of being; that conclusion being that he must be true to his own freedom and the actualization of this freedom over everything which is around him and in him. The permanent *crisis* into which he is forced by the permanent experience of anxiety arouses in him a permanent uneasiness and concern about his existential freedom of choice in this world.

At the same time, nausea, the ontological experience of being, teaches him the gratuitous arbitrariness, meaninglessness and groundlessness of everything that merely is. In the world of being, nothing can be anything else than it is. Every situation is merely a situation; it is, and signifies nothing. It could just as well be the exact opposite of what it is. The authentic man can thus never be satisfied with the contingent state of affairs in which he finds himself and experiences himself. Nor may he approve of it; it faces him as the alien and absurd and continual opponent.

One condition for a thorough-going honoring of these basic experiences is that man must rid himself completely of his belief in God. He *can* do this if he only realizes how man's misleading belief in God "actually" arose. He *must* do this, since belief in God is an impermissable obstacle to giving full honor to the experiences of freedom and contingency.

It is particularly an obstacle to the full honoring of the anxiety which reveals to us our freedom. This experience of anxiety also reveals to us that there is nothing *above* man. Man's freedom is foundational. His freedom is the one source of every norm and value.

The fear of God, Sartre says explicitly, is the opposite of the acknowledgment of man's own freedom, and is in principle a self-alienation of man. Sartre thus had his character Orestes complain to Jupiter that if Jupiter makes him follow Jupiter's orders, Jupiter is enslaving him. In the name of freedom, Orestes denies Jupiter the right to do this. In the name of humanity, "God" must disappear. Turning away from God is a prerequisite for acknowledging our own sovereignty. No humanism is possible without atheism. The apotheosis of man results in the disappearance of Jupiter, the "death of God."

Anxiety, the revelation of our own ontological freedom, thus teaches us that God *cannot* exist, and that belief in God *may not* exist.

The authentic man, he who does himself justice, is the atheistic man.

But the ontological experience of the contingency of being also reveals to us infallibly that God cannot exist and that belief in God may not exist. For a belief in the *creation* of the world is directly opposed to our experience of the meaningless and the chaotic lack of structure which there is in the world of being. Belief in creation demands the acceptance of a foundational basis for all being. And thus Christianity denies the "revelation" given us by our ontological experience of being: nausea.

Belief in God conflicts with acceptance of Nothingness and Being as basic structures; and hence it also conflicts with our infallible experiences of Being and Nothingness, of Contingency and Freedom.

The authentic man thus purges himself of belief in God as impossible and objectionable. Man's *self-being*, hand in hand with *disbelief* in reality (which is contingent and meaningless), roots out all belief in God. If there is belief in God, there can be no belief in *être* and *néant;* and if there is belief in *être* and *néant,* there can be no belief in God.

But we are not left facing this choice as if facing a dilemma. For the choice between the two is not difficult. Belief in God, says Sartre, can be explained as a view of man which is unworthy of man. It can be exposed as such; exposed as *treason* and as an *attack* on his own true human being.

This exposure Sartre reckons as part of his task. Naturally, he undertakes this "exposure" by using the "light" of our so-called infallible ontological experiences of freedom and contingency.

The *idea of God* can originate in more than one way, he says.

One way is the way in which it arises in Descarte's philosophy. Descartes thought of God as the absolutely Free, who "invents" goodness and truth on the ground of his freedom. Well, this idea of God must have originated in Descarte's intuitive experience of his own freedom and autonomy. He then hypostatizes this experience of freedom into "God," and thus projects in "God" what actually characterizes and belongs to man. Man, who really is creating and creative freedom. Hence the theology of Descartes is completely "understandable," and is "actually" anthropology, the projected self-knowledge of man.

Another way in which the idea of God can arise, closely akin to the former, is seen by examining the idea of God as his own foundation, his own basis, his own ground of being, the unity of *pour-soi* and *en-soi;* as a *pour-soi* that is a *pour-soi,* freedom, and as *en-soi,* being. This idea of God is also understandable, and indeed can be easily exposed as the projection of man's ideal picture of himself; man, who must be his own nihilating ground, has hypostatized his "pursuit of illusion" as an idea of God.

A third way in which the idea of God has originated is through the projection and hypostatization of the idea of "being objectivized by the other." This is primarily sensed by us through the other's glance, through "being seen" by the other; his glance can rest on me. Well, expanding this idea to its widest extent, it becomes "men can see me." And this notion, projected and hypostatized, becomes "God sees me." Thus the idea of God can arise as the infinite extension of the possible dispossession of the self, the possible dispossession of our own freedom.

But then the idea of God can mean only this, an attempt on our part to flee our own freedom and responsibility, to mask them, and to find an excuse for our flight. And the more *understandable* the origin of the idea of God becomes to anyone who accepts the infallible ontological experiences of Sartre's existentialism, the more *objectionable* any belief in God must become for him. Belief in God justifies the man who refuses to honor freedom and contingency; it justifies a false idea of self and a false idea of being; it justifies the false flight from man's freedom and responsibility into a self-enslavement, and justifies the flight from the actual world of contingency into a pseudo-ordered world of pseudo-law, which man need no longer nihilate but which he must rather respect. Belief in God gives man a false certainty that being has a right to be and a reason for "being." It robs man of the dynamic of his call to action and creation, creation of self and creation of a cosmos. It gives him the false idea that our heart is restless until it *finds rest* in God; actually, our heart is restless because it senses and vainly pursues rest in *itself*.

For Sartre, the authentic existential man is the guardian of humanity, and *therefore* the enemy of belief in God. Sartre's existentialism is an anti-theistic and anti-Christian humanism. He blames the philosophers of the Enlightenment for not having destroyed Christianity root and branch. Alas, they kept many remnants of Christianity, for they continued to believe as good rationalists in an objective order of values which are independent of man and thus limit man's freedom and place man under authority. The Enlightenment did not realize that man is the existential-creative source of all values and law. These remnants, says Sartre, must be demolished in the name of existentialism and thus in the name of humanity. Then and only then will there be room for the full acknowledgement of the practical application of the basic structures of human being, which are freedom and contingency, and the tension between them. Only then will the true human "being" of man become possible.

This anti-theistic and anti-Christian humanism "exposes" Christian belief, belief in God, as the flight of man from his own freedom and responsibility, as an apostasy from his own humaness, as a flight from the absurdity of reality, in which man lives with his existential tensions. Sartre sees himself as the apologist for true humanism, and as such he can be nothing else than the enemy of every belief in God.

The way is then clear for authentic and unfalsified human being; for man's "conversion" from his "attitude" of bad faith. Man's authentic being is characterized by a resolute and free acceptance of the necessity of the situative manner of existence which is man's. It is characterized by a life which builds forth, between nihilating freedom and the clearly realized illusion of a useless striving, towards man's self-actualization and self-salvation from the fetters of contingency. Builds, until death puts an end to the process, an absurd end.

There are no specific directrices for this task of self-realization, nor should there be. For such specific guidance would destroy the existential tension, cramp the act of freedom, and violate man's freedom of choice. The choice for choosing, the self-isolation of the inner act — these must be respected and hallowed. The ontological foundational project of man's own transcendence of being must be kept safe through the crisis-experience of anxiety; in order that man may live in the uncertainty of his free choices and in the danger of the unreckonable and intractable situations which loom up before him; so that he may be completely left to himself without excuse, without justification, with nothing to hold to; sovereign and helpless.

Man's authentic existence is threatened not only by belief in God but also, and continually, by the individual's neighbor. Every neighbor by the mere fact of his being there poses a threat to my authenticity, and is a seduction to self-betrayal and reason, a means of masking this self-treason.

The neighbor can do nothing else than try to dispossess me and subjugate me to himself. If I do not transcend this attempt of my neighbor, then I *misuse* my freedom, and become subjugated to him. For he cannot subjugate me unless I misuse my freedom and, in *bad faith* to myself, allow myself to be subjugated. He can then rule over me, because I put myself at his command. In this way I can twist the social conflict — the basic structure of all polytheistic society — into peaceful co-existence. But this peace can and must be exposed as self-betrayal and seduction. For I surely do not honor my freedom when I refuse to use it to launch the existential encounter with the outside world, but rather misuse it to let the power of the other prevail. I am untrue to myself; I let my neighbor be my hell, but I am no longer his.

This self-betrayal finds a place, above all, in everyday life, "normal" life. Whenever man conforms to public opinion, cooperates in a common effort, gives in to mode and convention, bourgeois life, tradition, social order — when he does this, he renounces his duty and calling to an anarchism based on principle. Man is then actually in flight from himself, and seeking a safe refuge in "men." He lets his freedom clot and stiffen and moulder, so to speak, through this false existential relationship, which takes a false middle ground between the actualizing of freedom and identity with being, between the empty and the full, between self and being; he lets being dominate his existence, and he lives non-authentically.

This is the average relationship of the average man. He is continually in bad faith to himself, untrue to himself.

He is not true to himself, to his own necessary revolt against contingent being. He uses his self-choosing in order to avoid choosing, freedom to avoid being free, responsibility to avoid being responsible, self-isolation in order to avoid isolation. He is at the same time deceiver and deceived. And he knows this. He cannot escape the ontological revelation of freedom and contingency. Immersion in the world, immersion in the deified results of our own or others' culture, immersion in social stability and comfortability — all of these are a self-betrayal of the individual in the "we," the crowd; and they must be unmasked and exposed as self-betrayal.

Sartre in his philosophy calls man back from his many forms of flight by jerking the mask from his face, and letting him see how he is fleeing from himself, fleeing from himself as freedom and anxiety and responsibility, fleeing from himself as the *indispensable*, the self called to auto-eroticism. Sartre lets man see how he flees from freedom and contingency by viewing future plans as accomplished facts, just as if he did not actually have to choose freely over and over, but could count on a comfortable determinism; as if no freedom and contingency existed. Sartre jerks off the mask from the pursuit of science, the weighty concerns over trifles, the "honorable" wish to be what man "is" (whereas man is actually *not* what he is), the petrification and objectivizing of the individual by the other, from society and its modes and mores and conventions, man's restless identification of himself with his own body, from belief in God with its false certainty, which relieves man from his basic responsibilities; from the daily jobs and successes, the daily tasks and certainties, from the pragmatic way of life.

The man of bad faith is also in flight from the two ontological foundationing experiences, anxiety and nausea; and from that which they reveal, freedom and contingency. He is a traitor. A traitor to himself, and as such a man who commits the deadly sin of attacking humanity.

Sartre's philosophy exposes these different ways of life as nonexistential, as flights, in order that man might turn from them to obedience to the truly human experiences of anxiety and nausea, and accept what they reveal about freedom and contingency and about the authentic existential encounter between them. Thus Sartre is a prophet of repentance, and his existentialism is a radical and atheistic humanist's call to repentance, who in ultra-modern form calls man to salvation — to self-salvation.

Sartre is the modern evangelist of freedom and contingency, of man's glory and importance, the evangelist who calls "us" from our sins, from our decadent religious and social life, from culture-building which is not crisis-building, from our self-alienation which is so unworthy of man; and Sartre has a basic belief on which the whole of his teaching rests; the so-called ontological experience of the self and of being. This, says Sartre, is infallible, and experienced by all men. And he makes this decree final by stamping it with a new decree — that anyone who refuses to follow these experience really knows better and is acting against his better knowledge.

I can hardly omit pointing out here Sartre's far-reaching *intolerance* of those who think and believe differently than he does. And also that Sartre's modernistic brand of intolerance is itself a mask; a mask for the *irreligious* sources from which his outlook on life and vision of life are assembled.

Nor is it an effective mask, for it is very easy to distinguish between religious thought and the anti-religious and anti-Christian character of Sartre's teaching. Anyone who compares the decisive words and ideas of Sartre's thought with the language of the Bible and of Christian belief can easily see this for himself.

Sartre's teaching is thus irreligious and it is indeed a tissue of plagiarism and perversion of religious ideas. His idea of freedom is a perversion of the sovereignty of God, his idea of self-election, a perversion of God's election, the idea of inter-human society as conflict, a borrowing from ancient polytheism, his idea of self-foundationing man taken from the *aseitas* of God, who is his own foundation.

His idea of the power of freedom is a humanistic counterpart of the Occamistic idea of God, his idea of man's project of self-salvation a travesty on the gospel, his teaching on contingency an adulterated reproduction of divine creation (and also the checkmate to freedom's power). His cult of man's self-worship is a twisted version of divine worship; his teaching on society, a radicalization of this cult of self to include the subjugation of one's neighbor; his existential tension corresponds to divine leading and ruling; his salvation the walling-in of man behind the barriers of auto-eroticism; his idea of man in flight before God; and his deepest intent is an apostate *Eritis sint Deus,* you shall be as God, by forsaking God and justifying that which the Bible teaches as the fall into sin.

Sartre's anti-religious teaching is so deeply steeped in anti-religious principle that he never even for a moment examines with a critical eye the basis of his own dogmatic assumptions. He excuses himself from this task — the duty of every philosopher, and indeed every man — by his arbitrary decree that the ontological experiences on which his philosophy is based are infallible.

This is a wholly gratuitous assumption. And it is one which will be opposed as long as the antithesis of Sartrian existentialism encounters the thesis of Christian belief embodied in living Christians.